A YOUNG GIRL'S JOURNEY TO FREEDOM
CHALLENGING FAITH

THE STORY OF **RUTH SIMON HEINEMANN**
AS TOLD TO HER DAUGHTER

Susan Heinemann Berman

This book is a work of nonfiction. The events and experiences portrayed here are based on the recollections of Ruth (Simon) Heinemann and Edith (Simon) Babich and are presented as truthfully as memory permits. All persons within are actual individuals. The author recognizes that the memories or impressions of the events and experiences described here may be different than how any of the characters in the book or other readers may have remembered or experienced them.

Most of the conversations in the book come from Ruth (Simon) Heinemann's and Edith (Simon) Babich's own recollections, though they are not written to represent word-for-word transcripts of such conversations unless they are indicated as such. Some dialogue consistent with the situation or nature of the people speaking has been recreated because it is almost impossible to recall every word of a conversation. The author has retold them in a way that evokes the feeling and meaning of what was said and, in all instances, the essence of the dialogue is accurate.

The material in this book was not intended to harm any individual or the general public's impression of such persons, but rather as a way to present Ruth (Simon) Heinemann's and Edith (Simon) Babich's experience as honestly as possible. The author recognizes that there are particular truths that are essential to the telling of this story and regrets any unintentional harm resulting from the publishing and marketing of *Challenging Faith*.

Printed in the United States of America

Last digit is print number 10 9 8 7 6 5 4 3 2

DEDICATION

This book is dedicated to my family—past, present, and future.

To our loving parents, Selma and Karl Simon, thank you for all you did to make our lives special and to protect us from harm. You were very brave in the face of danger.

To our dear departed sister, Ilse, although your life was cut tragically short, your memory and sacrifices, along with our parents, have not been forgotten. They live on in each and every member of this family and especially in one of our newest members named Ilse, after you.

To my late beloved sisters, Edith and Hilde, of blessed memory, this book was written for all of us. It tells our stories before, during, and after the war and the Holocaust and how we survived.

We are very grateful for the opportunity America afforded us to make new lives and raise our wonderful families.

To my late loving husband, Fred, and his family; our late beloved son, Gary; our two wonderful daughters, Susan and Julie, and their loving husbands, Steve and Rich; and my grandchildren, David, Daniel and wife, Betsy; and my sweet great grandson, Finn ... I share this remembrance with all of you. I hope this makes you proud of the family you were born into or acquired. I love you all very much, along with the rest of our family, and keep you in my prayers each day.

A special thanks to my eldest daughter, Susan, who through her diligence and hard work made this book a dream come true for me.

May this testament serve to impart our families' spirit and dedication to G'd and to Judaism for all who read it. Let our history live on and be a *lesson to educate every human being that hatred and bigotry cause unnecessary pain, loss and suffering to everyone including the perpetrators.*

With a full heart,
Ruth Simon Heinemann

CONTENTS

FOREWORD

In March 2008 I led a congregational trip to Israel from Temple Beth Kodesh—a Conservative synagogue located in Boynton Beach, FL. Among the 20 travelers was an 83-year-old woman, a Holocaust survivor by the name of Ruth Heinemann. Aside from wanting to experience Israel, Ruth had another reason for going. This was made clear when we visited Yad Vashem—Israel's memorial to the victims of the Shoah.

While the rest of the group was touring Yad Vashem, I accompanied Ruth to meet with one of their staffers. Why? Because Ruth wanted to give her some papers and photos—information on her family who had perished during the Shoah. She wanted there to be a file on them so that their lives would be remembered.

When we left that office, Ruth had a smile and an expression of satisfaction on her face; as if many worries had been lifted from her shoulders. I asked her why she felt that way. She replied that this was something that she felt she had an obligation to do and she has fulfilled that obligation.

The story of how Ruth Heinemann arrived at that point in her life is told in the following pages of this book. As you will read, it is a life shaped by many traumatic events, including living through Kristallnacht, going to England on the Kindertransport, finding out her parents and sisters were on the ill-fated ship the MS St. Louis, and finally coming to America and raising a family.

Through it all, Ruth always strived to maintain her steadfast faith. This is the story of Ruth Simon Heinemann's *Challenging Faith*.

Rabbi Michael C. Simon

Rabbi Simon is the Spiritual leader of Temple Beth Kodesh in Boynton Beach, FL and was Ruth's rabbi during her many years there. More information can be found at: www.TempleBethKodesh.org.

He is also the author of *The Blue and White Road: A Path To a Fulfilling Jewish Life.*

INTRODUCTION

The Story of Ruth Simon Heinemann
as told to her daughter, Susan Heinemann Berman

When my mother, Ruth Heinemann, asked me to write her life story, I was flattered; but also anxious to make it as accurate and concise as possible. I wanted it to reflect her personality and to be worthy of the confidence that she had placed in me.

As her elder daughter, I have been privileged to know and love her all my life. I've seen her evolve from a young mother and house-wife to her many roles as a mentor, a woman of deep commitment, and a leader among her friends. She has been a wonderful mother, daughter, sister, and grandmother, as well as a supportive confidante to many generations of our family.

My cousins and their children keep in regular contact with her and value her input and advice. She is very interested in sharing their lives since she is the matriarch of the family. In addition, she main-tains many relationships amongst former neighbors and friends from Illinois to Florida, and beyond.

My sister, Julie, and I value Mom's influence and opinion too, but do not live in her shadow. She has shown us time and time again how to stand up for ourselves as women, as Jews, as Americans, and as car-ing individuals of this universe. Her inspiration knows no bounds!

Mom has been through much trauma in her life, but displays great determination and courage. She is 97½ years young and con-tinues to strive for a full and active life with her children, her grand-children, and now her first great-grandson. She is well respected in her community, and prides herself in participating in many activi-ties, including chair aerobics, each day.

My mother is also a survivor of the Holocaust, which is a testa-ment to her faith that she admits has wavered at times, but has never been broken.

I pray that we are allowed to enjoy her for many more years to come in good health and that she maintains her "zest for life"!!!

With humble appreciation,
Susan Heinemann Berman

(Maternal) Katz Family Tree

Jacob Katz, b. 7/9/1863 in Helsen, Germany, d. 9/29/1925 Arolsen, Germany

> m. Ida on 1/8/1894 in Kassel, Germany.
Ida Schartenberg Katz, b. 1/31/1873 in Zierenberg, Germany, d. in a Nazi camp in 1943 in Theresienstadt Transit Camp (no definitive record)
(Ida's parents were Moses Schartenberg and Sara (Israel) Schartenberg)

They had the following children:

+ *Selma Sina (Katz) Simon,* b. 12/27/1894 in Arolsen, Germany, d. 5/21/1943 in Sobibor Concentration Camp in Lubelskie, Poland
  > m. Karl Simon on 11/25/1918 in Arolsen, Germany
  ↳ They had 4 daughters: Edith (Simon) Babich, Ruth (Simon) Heinemann, Hildegard Hanna (Simon) Gernsheimer, and Ilse Simon (see other pages for details of their births and deaths)

+ *Helene (Katz) Ries,* b. 3/4/1896 in Arolsen, Germany, d. 5/11/1995 in Jacksonville, FL
  > m. Abraham (Arthur) Ries on 7/27/1920 in Bad-Arolsen, Germany [b. 12/24/1885 in Bunde, Germany, d. 10/18/1944 in Auschwitz Concentration Camp]
  ↳ Ernest Moritz Ries, b. 1/22/1922 in Bunde, Germany, d. 3/25/1989 in Dallas, TX
    > m. Betty Maxine (Samet) Ries on 1/29/1956 [b. 9/28/1925 in Atlanta, GA, d. 7/13/1980 in Dallas, TX]
    ⇢ They had 2 children: David (married, 1 child) and Patty
    > m. Myrna Faith (Zapruder) Ries in Dallas, TX on 8/1/1982

+ *Martha (Katz) Stern,* b. 9/30/1897 in Arolsen, Germany, d. 1940 in a concentration camp in Poland
  > m. Ferdinand Stern on 3/11/1921 in Bad-Arolsen, Germany [b. 10/16/1890 in Bad Zwesten, Germany, d. 11/14/1938 in Buchenwald Concentration Camp]
  ↳ Helmut Stern, b. 2/16/1922 in Marburg, Germany, d. 5/10/2002 in Deltona, FL
  ↳ Manfred Stern b. 6/4/1923, d. in a concentration camp
  ↳ Lieselotte (Lilo) (Stern) Waxman, b. 3/19/1925 in Frankenberg, Germany, d. 10/7/2010 in Miami, FL
    > m. Rabbi Alfred A. Waxman on 8/13/1944 in Leeds, England
    ⇢ They had 2 children: Martha and Faith. They each married and had 2 children; Martha has 4 grandchildren and Faith has 2 grandchildren.
  ↳ Richard Stern, b. 1/9/1932, d. in a concentration camp
  ↳ Heinz Stern, 9/2/1936, d. in a concentration camp

+ *Max Katz*, b. 2/11/1900 in Arolsen, Germany, d. 10/1/1944 in Riga Concentration Camp

  > m. Bertel (Bertha) Julie (Stern) Katz on 5/2/1927 in Osnabruck, Germany [b. 2/15/1905 in Niedersachsen, Germany, d. 10/1/1944 in Riga Concentration Camp]

+ *Else (Katz) Meyerhoff*, b. 12/7/1903 in Arolsen, Germany, d. 12/11/1996 in Jacksonville, FL

  > m. Albert Meyerhoff on 5/12/1925 in Arolsen, Germany [b. 6/3/1899 in Volkmarsen, Germany, d. 8/3/1973 in Jacksonville, FL]

  ↳ Gertrude (Meyerhoff) Bobroff, b. 8/3/1926 in Arolsen, Germany, d. 8/21/2009 in Gainesville, FL

     > m. Alvin Bobroff in Jacksonville, FL 1/9/1949 [b. 7/20/1922 in Jacksonville, FL, d. 3/1/2008 in Gainesville, FL]

     ⇥ They had 3 children: Steven, Jean, and Larry. Steven married, had 1 child and has 2 grandchildren. Jean married, and Larry married and is deceased

  ↳ Eric Meyerhoff, b. 3/20/1929 in Arolsen, Germany, d. 5/2020 in Savannah, GA

     > m. Harriet (Cranman) Meyerhoff in Savannah, GA on 9/9/1973 [b. 6/1946 in Savannah, GA]

     ⇥ They had 2 children: Margot and Mark (they are both married).

+ *Siegried Israel Katz*, b. 7/1/1905 Arolsen, Germany, d. 1/10/1916 Arolsen, Germany

+ *Meinhard Katz*, b. 7/1/1906 Arolsen, Germany, d. 7/17/1992 Jacksonville, FL

  > m. Dora (Gross) Katz 11/3/1946 in Jacksonville, FL [b. 5/23/1916 in Baltimore, MD, d. 10/11/2003 Jacksonville, FL]

  ↳ Charles Max Katz, b. 1952. Charles married and had 2 children.

(PATERNAL) SIMON FAMILY TREE

SIMON SIMON, B. 4/23/1855 IN BERGE, GERMANY, D. 8/25/1932 IN WERTLE, GERMANY

> m. Sophie in Wertle, Germany

Sophie Frank Simon, b. 10/9/1859 in Wertle, Germany (date of death and location unknown)

(Sophie's parents were Leser and Hanna Frank)

They had the following children:

+ *Karl Simon*, b. 7/5/1884 in Wertle, Germany, d. 5/21/1943 in Sobibor Concentration Camp

  > m. Selma Sina (Katz) Simon, b. 5/27/1894, d. 5/21/1943 in Sobibor Concentration Camp

  ↳ They had 4 daughters: Edith (Simon) Babich, Ruth (Simon) Heinemann, Hildegard (Simon) Hanna Gernsheimer, and Ilse Simon (see other pages for details of their births and deaths)

+ *Helene (Simon) Meyer*, b. 8/1/1886, d. after December 1941 in Riga Ghetto, Latvia

  > m. Max Meyer

  ↳ They had 3 children: Grete & Hans (twins) and Ernst Meyer

  ↳ Grete, b. 12/10/1910 in Herzlake, Germany, d. 8/4/1978 in Hartford, CT

  → m. Rudy Weinberg

  → They had 1 son named Mark (b. 1952). Mark married and had 3 children, each is married and has 1 child.

  ↳ Hans, b. 12/10/1910 in Herzlake, Germany, d. 1985 in Israel

  → Hans married, moved to Israel, and had 1 son—Dror

  ↳ Ernst (changed his name to Michael Kelly during the war), b. 9/6/1919 Herzlake, Germany, d. 4/28/2006 Roslyn, NY

  → m. Gertrude (Trudie) (Benger) Kelly 9/5/1948 in St. John Woods, London [b. 4/22/1922 in Vienna, Austria, d. 2/2009 in Roslyn, New York]

  → They had 3 children: Vera, Diana, and Jerry (twins) married. Vera [b. 1950] has 2 children, 3 grandchildren and 1 great grandchild; Diana [b. 1955] has 3 children; Jerry [b. 1955] is married with no children.

+ *Rika (Simon) Frank*, b. 3/9/1888 in Wertle, Germany, d. 1/29/1933 in Quakenbruck, Germany

  > m. Karl Frank

  ↳ They had 1 child named Benjamin (Benno) b. 1912 in Quakenbruck, Germany. Benno moved to South Africa and married. He has 1 child.

- *Leser Simon*, b. 12/14/1889 in Wertle, Germany, d. 1/23/1935 in Wertle, Germany
  - m. Fanny Simon
    - ↳ They had 2 children: Hugo and Sonya. Neither of them survived the war.
- *Fritz Simon*, b. 10/23/1893 in Wertle, Germany, d. 8/18/1916 in World War I
- *Else (Simon) Gerson*, b. 12/1/1895, d. 10/11/1944 in KZ Auschwitz Concentration Camp
  - m. Abraham Gerson in Bunde, Germany [b. 10/12/1876 in Bunde, Germany, d. 8/22/1931 in Bunde, Germany]
    - ↳ They had 1 child named Betty (Gerson) Herman [b. 12/15/1920 in Bunde, Germany, d. 3/8/1992 in Reading, PA]
      - ⇢ Betty married Henry Herman in 1944 in Westerbork Transit Camp in Assen, Netherlands [b. 11/4/1914 in Euskirchen, Germany, d. 4/1/1994 in Reading, PA]
      - ⇢ They had 3 children: Franklin, b. 1947, d. 1948; Dennis, b. 1950, d. 2020; Ellen (Herman) Azrael b. 1951. She married and has 1 child.
- *Emilie Milly (Simon) Shaap*, b. 11/11/1898 in Wertle, Germany, d. 10/29/1942 in Lesser, Poland
  - m. Bendix Sharp [b. 5/13/1892 in Lathen, Germany, d. 12/1/1942 in Lesser, Poland (Holocaust)]
    - ↳ They had 4 children: Egon, August, Sonia, and Fritz (none of them survived the war)
      - ⇢ Egon, b. 1922, d. 6/21/1939 in Lathen, Germany
      - ⇢ August, b. 1926, d. 12/9/1942 in Lesser, Poland
      - ⇢ Sonia, b. 1929, d. 10/29/1942 in Lesser, Poland
      - ⇢ Fritz, b. 1931, d. 10/29/1942 in Lesser, Poland

There appears to have been two other children that were born to Simon Simon and his beloved wife Sophie (Frank) Simon. They lived abbreviated lives. They were:

- *Adele Simon*, b. 1892 in Wertle, Germany, d. 11/28/1894 in Wertle, Germany
- *Moritz Simon*, b. 1901 in Wertle, Germany, d. 11/12/1906 in Wertle, Germany

KARL AND SELMA SIMON

Karl Simon	Married	Selma (Katz) Simon
b. 7/5/1884	11/25/1918	b. 12/27/1894
d. 5/21/1943 in Lubelskie,	Arolsen	d. 5/21/1943 in Lubelskie,
Poland, Sobibor		Poland, Sobibor
Concentration Camp		Concentration Camp

They had 4 children (see below for more details):

↳ *Edith Simon*, b. 7/1/1922 in Cloppenburg, Germany, d.10/16/2005 in Pompano Beach, FL

↳ *Ruth Simon*, b. 2/25/1925 in Cloppenburg, Germany

↳ *Hildegard Hanna Simon*, b. 5/2/1926 in Quakenbruck, Germany, d. 3/27/2019 in Wyomissing, PA

↳ *Ilse Simon*, b. 3/8/1928 in Quakenbruck, Germany, d. 5/21/1943 in Lubelskie, Poland, Sobibor Concentration Camp

Edith (Simon) Babich	Married	Reuben Babich
b. 1922, d. 2005	7/1945	b. 1923, d. 2021
	Brooklyn, NY	

They had 3 children:

↳ Sandra Babich, b. 1946

   ➤ m. Jan Lazarus in 1967. Jan died in 1990.

   ⇢ They had 2 children and 4 grandchildren.

   ⇢ Sandra (Babich) Lazarus remarried. She married Barry Keller in 1994. She is now Sandra (Babich) Lazarus Keller.

↳ Karen Sue Babich, b. 1949

   ⇢ Karen was married and had 1 son. She is now married to Marty Schlisky. Karen has 6 grandchildren.

↳ Janice (Babich) Howe, b. 1951

   ⇢ Janice was married and had 2 children. She now has 5 grandchildren.

Ruth (Simon) Heinemann	Married	Manfred Heinemann
b. 1925	3/47	b. 1922, d. 2001
	Brooklyn, NY	

They had 3 children:

↳ Susan Marion Heinemann, b. 1948

   ➤ m. Steven Berman in 1969 in Framingham, MA

   ⇢ They have 2 children:

     ¤ David A. Berman, b. 1971

     ¤ Daniel I. Berman, b. 1975; m. Betsy Steed in 2018 and have 1 child

↳ Gary Phillip Heinemann, b. 1954, d. 2010
⇢ Gary was never married.
↳ Julie Ann Heinemann, b. 1963
⇢ m. Richard Powsner (b. 1960 in New York, NY) in 1989 in Raleigh, NC

Hildegard (Simon) Gernsheimer	Married	*Solly Gernsheimer*
b. 1926, d. 2019	3/1946	b. 1912, d. 1987
	Brooklyn, NY	

They had 3 children:
↳ Jacob Simon Gernsheimer, b. 1946, d. 2021
> m. Amy (White) Gernsheimer 1969-1987. They had 2 children.
⇢ Jack and Amy's son predeceased them and their daughter was married with 3 children.
> m. Nancy E. Wolff in 1990 in Bernville, PA
↳ Jeffry Charles Gernsheimer, b. 1946
> m. Jan (Barnett) Gernsheimer in 1980 and they have 2 children
⇢ Jeff was Jack's identical twin.
↳ Sharon Lois Gernsheimer, b. 1951
⇢ m. Barry Levine in 1990 and they have 2 children—fraternal twins
✦ Hilde married Manfred Jakobs in 1999 in Reading, PA. He died in 2006.

JULIUS FRANK, SECOND COUSIN OF KARL SIMON

JULIUS FRANK, B. 12/18/1895 IN WERTLE, GERMANY, D. 7/1981 FORRESTON, IL

Julius was known to the Simon girls as Uncle Julius (and his wife was Tante Selma).

Julius was the son of Victor Frank and Helene/Serle Lina Frank.

Julius was the brother of: Julchen, Samuel, Alex, Ella Edel Heilbronn, Mortiz (Morris), Leopold, Frieda Samson, and Johanna ten Brink.
> m. Selma (Lazarus) Frank [b. 9/3/1902, d. 11/1975 in Forreston, IL] (Selma was the daughter of Isaac Lazarus and Julchen Frank)
↳ Julius and Selma's loving son, Gunther, was born in 1930 in Germany.
> Gunther married Inge Lazarus in 1961 in IL [b. 1937 in Cloppenburg, d. 2015 in Chicago, IL]. (Inge was the daughter of Gerda [Oppenheimer] and Alex Lazarus.)
⇢ They had 2 children: Mark Frank [b. 1959] and Steven Frank [b. 1962]. Each son married and had 3 children. Mark has 2 grandchildren.

HEINEMANN FAMILY TREE

SALI HEINEMANN, B. 4/22/1891 IN OBERELSBACH, GERMANY, D. 6/1/1967 IN BROOKLYN, NEW YORK

(Sali's father's name was Fritz Heinemann)

➤ m. Sabina Heinemann in Treuchtlingen, Germany
Sabina (Freiman) Heinemann b. 1/1/1896 in Treuchtlingen, Germany, d. 6/1971 in Freeport, IL
(Sabina was the daughter of Phillip and Pauline Freiman)

They had the following children:

✦ *Manfred Heinemann*, b. 8/7/1922 in Treuchtlingen, Germany, d. 6/26/2001 in Boynton Beach, FL

➤ m. Ruth (Simon) Heinemann on 3/23/1947 in Brooklyn, NY
↳ Susan (Heinemann) Berman, b. 1948 Brooklyn, NY.
➤ m. Steven Neil Berman 6/8/1969 in Framingham, MA. Steven is the son of Isidore and Goldie Berman from New York, NY. Steve was born in New York, NY in 1946.
⇢ Susan and Steve had 2 children: David Adam Berman and Daniel Isadore Berman. Daniel wed Betsy Steed 9/2018 in Callicoon, New York; they have 1 child.
↳ Gary Phillip Heinemann, b. 1954 in Brooklyn, NY, d. 2010 Schoharie, NY. He was never married.
↳ Julie Ann (Heinemann) Powsner, b. 1963 in Framingham, MA
➤ m. Richard Powsner 9/9/1989 in Raleigh, NC. Richard is the son of Norman and Barbara Powsner of Long Island, NY. Richard was born in New York, NY in 1960.

✦ *Harry N. Heinemann,* b. 12/1933 in Treuchtlingen, Germany d. 4/2022 Great Neck, NY

➤ m. Susan Rae (Turk) Heinemann 7/3/1958 in Brooklyn, New York. Susan (b. 7/1937 in New York, NY) is the daughter of Abraham and Esther Turk.
↳ Richard Heinemann
➤ m. Laura McClure 8/1988 in Chicago, IL. (Laura is the daughter of Charles McClure and Miriam [Daum] Selby.)
⇢ Richard and Laura had Nickolas, Jakob, and Gabriel. Jakob married Hannah (Anderson) Heinemann 6/2022 in Madison, WI.

1
Life in Cloppenburg

Ruth Heinemann (*nee* Simon) was born at home with the help of a midwife on February 25, 1925 (Figure 1-1). She was the second of four daughters that Karl and Selma (*nee* Katz) Simon would welcome to their family. Edith, Ruth's older sister, had been delivered in the same manner in their home in Cloppenburg, Germany a little over two and a half years earlier.

The younger daughters, Hildegard and Ilse, were born in a nearby hospital in the town of Quakenbruck. Hilde was just fifteen months younger than Ruth, and Ilse was two years younger than Hilde. Little Ilse completed their family upon her arrival on March 8, 1928.

Karl and Selma had come from much larger families—they each had six siblings and was the oldest child in their family. Karl was raised in Werlte (pronounced Velta), and Selma in the town of Bad Arolsen, which was some six hours away. They might never have met had Karl's little sister, Else, not been looking out for him. Else met Selma in a third community, where they became friends at the finishing school they both attended. She introduced Selma to her big brother Karl, and they were married on November 25, 1918 in Selma's hometown.

Karl's father, Simon Simon, had a general store in Werlte, in addition to being a horse and cattle dealer (Figure 1-2). Karl's mother, Sophie Frank, and he had known each other for several years before they started courting.

Each spring the town of Wertle conducted an annual festival called Schutzenfest. One year as a young lad, Simon was chosen to be the King of the festival, which entitled him to pick a young maiden to be his Queen. He chose Sophie, and it wasn't too long after the festival that the King and Queen became engaged and were married!

Figure 1-1. Formal picture of Ruth's mother, Selma Simon, with Ruth age 9 months and Edith age 3 and half, circa 1925.

Selma's parents were Jacob and Ida (*nee* Schartenberg) Katz, and Selma's father traded and sold horses as well (Figure 1-3). They were quite successful, as were Karl's parents. In fact, Jacob supplied the Principality of Arolsen (which had a castle in the town and a Prince living in it) with the horses they required. Jacob also sold his steeds to many businesses and farmers throughout his community.

Figure 1-2. Formal picture of Simon Simon's immediate family. *Seated* (l-r): Simon Simon, Emilie (Milly), Sophie; *Standing* (l-r): Else, Karl, Rika, Fritz, Leser, and Helene.

Figure 1-3. Formal picture of Jacob Katz's immediate family. *Seated* (l-r): Ida, Else, Jacob, Max; *Standing* (l-r): Siegfried, Helene, Selma, Martha, and Meinhard.

Figure 1-4. The 1918 formal engagement portrait of Selma Katz.

Shortly after Karl and Selma's marriage (Figure 1-4), the two of them decided to move to a small town called Cloppenburg so Karl could take up cattle and horse dealing on his own. Cloppenburg lies in the Lower Saxony region, about 150 miles from the German border with Holland. It was mostly an agricultural community and was predominantly Catholic. However, there were eventually nine Jewish families that settled in the town, and they were able to build a Conservative synagogue and operate their own Jewish cemetery.

Karl became a prosperous livestock dealer and was considered one of the finest gentlemen and businessmen in his field. He was a kind, honest, and well-respected man. Selma was a homemaker and ran the family's household very efficiently. She was also the disciplinarian of the family.

Ruth describes her siblings in this manner when they were children, all living in the same household together. Edith, the eldest, was a beautiful, tall, blonde, blue-eyed girl and looked more German than any of her sisters. She was fairly studious and very sweet. She had her own friends and didn't pay that much attention to her younger sisters. But, it was nice to know that she could be counted on if Ruth needed her advice or just to talk to.

Hilde, almost her "Irish" twin, was a good student and had a lot of common sense. She loved to play, but she was somewhat quiet and shy. There seemed to be some rivalry between the two. Each one of the middle daughters vied for attention among the other family members, so there were disagreements between them now and then.

Ilse, Ruth recalls, was a bit of a tomboy. She liked to climb trees and didn't worry too much about being ladylike. She was the "little sister". She didn't like thinking of herself in those terms though. She loved to hang out with her older sisters and be included in their activities.

It was quite a lively household. They had a nursemaid for a while when the girls were younger. Edith and Ilse each had their own rooms and the two middle ones, Hilde and Ruth, shared a bedroom.

They had a butcher who would come about once or twice a month to "kosher" meat and wursts. On occasion, there was one customer and his son that would spend the night because they came from a great distance to purchase horses, and had become personal favorites of Karl's. They were the Kellers; Max was the father and Joseph, the son.

The Jewish Sabbath begins at sundown on Friday, so on Saturday mornings the Simon family would attend services at their local synagogue. Then, often after an afternoon nap, their father would treat the girls to candy or ice cream. Karl would load the girls up in a carriage or maybe walk with them to a nearby store. Ruth and her sisters loved spending time with their father, who was easy going and fun to be around.

Ruth would sometimes go for a walk with one of her mother's friends on Sunday. Her companion would tell Ruth frequently that "she could do anything she set her mind to doing". On one occasion, the two of them happened to stroll by a construction site and Ruth said to her elder, "You said I could do anything, but I couldn't build a house like that!" Ruth said she must have caught the woman off guard because she did not have a reply. Ruth learned to speak her mind from that incident and, most of the time, it served her well.

Before the Nazis came to power, Ruth and her sisters led a normal life for young German girls growing up in their town. They attended a local parochial school ten minutes from their home, had many friends, and enjoyed a full family life. They wore little blue and white uniforms.

The school was taught by nuns, was well run, and had a fine reputation. It was considered one of the best schools in the region, and Hilde and Ruth walked to school together despite the fact that they were in different grades. There was a path behind their house that they would follow right to the school. Ilse would walk by herself to her classes later in the morning, and Edith went separately with some of her classmates. The girls were welcomed despite their Jewish faith. The administration did not require them to take religious instruction. The Simon sisters attended Hebrew School at their local synagogue, but occasionally they would visit other Jewish communities.

One winter's day when Ruth was about nine, the girls were treated to a ride through the snow on a large sleigh pulled by horses. She recalls they were all bundled up in blankets and their Stableman, Louie Averback, drove them to visit their father's cousin and family in Quakenbruck. There was a much larger Jewish population in that town, and they had such a good time singing Chanukah songs and lighting the menorah in the synagogue's social hall.

Ruth and Hilde loved horses. Since there were many in their father's stable, their father allowed his daughters to have a special one to ride on occasion, with permission. The horse was called Fuchs (pronounced "fooks"). He was a gentle soul and they treated him to lots of carrots and apples.

One day when Ruth was about 10 years of age, Louie had come home from a business trip. She met him at the stable door and asked if she could put away the horse and carriage for him. He said, "Sure." Then Ruth got the idea that instead of unharnessing the horse and so forth, that she would take a quick ride by herself so, she climbed aboard the carriage and off she went. In the recesses of her mind, she must have known she was going to get in trouble for doing it, so her conscience got the better of her at the end of her street. She turned around and headed back to the stable. Louie was looking for her when she arrived and was not happy. He never told her parents about the incident so she didn't get in "hot water", but it reflects her determination to do things on her own terms when it suited her.

Ruth and Hilde were frequently dressed alike as children because they were so close in age. Her mother would sometimes take Ruth into Oldenburg, the city closest to them, for doctors' appointments and then to look at dresses in the shops along the avenue. Selma would occasionally buy her second oldest a dress in one of those establishments and then search for similar material to have a seamstress make sister dresses for the rest of the girls.

The dressmaker came twice a year to their home, where she would stay with them for a week. The talented young woman enjoyed visiting with the Simons, and the evidence of her work can be seen in several photographs of the girls throughout this book and on the cover.

It was a wonderful life for the Simon family in Germany. They were part of a community that accepted them, they felt secure and, more importantly, they had one another.

2
Storm Clouds Brewing

Things started to change for the Simon family and the rest of the Jewish community with the election of Adolph Hitler around 1933. Hitler was a rather brash individual—not very well educated, but very ambitious. He was quite a persuasive orator, however. He appealed to those German citizens that felt frustrated that their country's economy, among other things, was in shambles.

Germany had lost WWI, and therefore had to capitulate to the victors. The German government was forced to sign the Treaty of Versailles, which required Germany to give up a considerable amount of land and pay heavy reparations to their former enemies.

Ever so slowly at first, and then with more brazenness, Hitler made the general German populace feel that he understood their pain and severe disappointment in their government having lost the fight. Germany had been taken advantage of, he insinuated, and good Germans had a right to be resentful. He started undermining Germany's government one step at a time and eventually took over as Chancellor of the country. And when President Paul Von Hindenberg died suddenly, Hitler became President by default.

The Führer (as he demanded to be called) needed a scapegoat, and so he blamed the Jews for much of Germany's ill fortune. After all, the Jews were the ones with all the money, he opined. He started passing edicts that chastised Jews and prevented them from attending local schools, enjoying parks, libraries, and other public facilities. Jews were forced to carry ID cards with a large "J" on them that stigmatized them from other German citizens. This led to much prejudice and anti-Semitism throughout the country.

Every few days more prejudicial laws were passed pitting the German government and the German populace at large against their German "Enemies of the State"—Jews, Communists, Romas (gypsies), the handicapped, and homosexuals.

Hitler established a youth force encouraging German children to spy upon their elders and others in the community and report on them if they saw anything nefarious. It became clear that things were getting increasingly more dangerous as time went on, particularly for Jews.

Karl and Selma were most concerned about the safety of their family and they decided that should they have to leave hastily, they would go to America. They had some family there already. They tried not to show their concern to the children, but the girls felt it, too.

The family and the Jewish community prayed that life would get better and they would be allowed to remain citizens of their homeland. They loved Germany. They were proud German citizens; their family had lived in Deutschland for generations, and even fought for it. One of Karl's brothers had died in WWI for his country. Another brother was injured and was awarded the Iron Cross (a medal of the highest distinction for bravery); he eventually succumbed to his injuries, as well. Karl believed that surely those losses would make a difference.

They were proud of their Jewish heritage, kept kosher, and prayed regularly to maintain their faith.

MEMORIES & ADJUSTMENTS

There were happier times along the way, even through the rough years. Ruth remembers a special celebration the girls prepared for their father when he turned 50 in July of 1934.

Figure 2-1. Hilde, Ilse, Edith, and Ruth holding a sign congratulating their father on his 50th birthday in July of 1934.

He had been out of town on a business trip, and when he arrived home he was proud to proclaim that he had purchased not one, but *two* handsome buggies for his family to enjoy. Their mother, Selma, was quite astonished at his extravagance, but the girls thought it was great! He was so thrilled to see all of them, felt their sentiments, and share in their joy. Figure 2-1 is a photo of all four sisters in their identical attire holding a sign that was made exclaiming, "We Congratulate You" in German.

But adjustments had to be made to adapt to a somewhat more challenging way of life as well. Once the law barring Jewish youth from attending their regular schools was enacted, one of the biggest concerns of Jewish parents was how and where their children could continue their formal education. The Rabbi of the Oldenburg synagogue, one of the largest Jewish communities in the region, called a meeting of the families in the area that would be affected.

It was agreed that a school of various grades would be established in Oldenburg and housed in a building adjacent to the synagogue. Ruth, Hilde, and Ilse were amongst those who would attend.

Edith was permitted to finish up at the parochial school (since she fell within the small percentage of Jewish students the law would allow in private schools). Upon graduation, Edith intended to go to a finishing school in Hamburg, and that is exactly what she ended up doing.

Ruth and Hilde were woken up at 5:30 am on school days in order to arrive at school for an 8:00 am class. Their journey entailed riding

Figure 2-2. Ruth, Hilde, Uncle Max and a horse in Arolsen during the summer of 1937.

their bicycles to the nearby Cloppenburg train station where they would then board the train to Oldenburg for approximately an hour's ride. Once they arrived in the city, they would then have to walk about a mile to get to their new school. Ilse followed the same routine, only she left for school early enough to arrive for a 9 am class with children her own age. The classes included general studies, some Hebrew and Jewish education, and even some rudimentary English.

Ruth believes the first year that they transferred to the Oldenburg Jewish school was the 1936/37 school year. That would have put the girls at ages 11, 10, and 8.

Despite the length of the trip each weekday to receive their formal education, they do remember some very good times from that year. During that summer, Hilde and Ruth went to Arolsen to visit their maternal grandmother, Ida Katz. It was about a five-hour train ride, so they stayed with her for several weeks. Figure 2-2 shows the girls and their Uncle Max.

They enjoyed their visit very much and remember visiting the nearby gardens of the Prince's castle. They gathered flowers and were able to have tea and feel like real princesses themselves. It was also an opportunity to see a different part of the country and to learn to be more independent. That December for Chanukah, there was a special surprise for the girls. Their parents enlisted the help of a young couple they knew and had them build a puppet theater so they could

Figure 2-3. Final formal portrait of the Simon family, circa 1937. *Seated* (l-r): Karl, Ruth, and Selma; *Standing* (l-r): Hilde, Edith and Ilse.

entertain the family with a live puppet show, similar to Punch and Judy. Everything was hidden in the attic for the show, but somehow, Ruth suspected something was afoot a few weeks before the surprise. So, she peeked in the attic one day just to satisfy her own curiosity. She saw the props, the costumes, and the stage but she dared not say anything to anyone because she would spoil the surprise and get in trouble. When the time came, she acted as delighted as the others because it was such a wonderful occasion (Figure 2-3).

Then there was her final birthday at home, February 25, 1938, when her parents gave her a beautiful doll. It had long brown hair, a beautiful pink dress, and, because they knew she had always wanted a doll like that, it carried that much more significance for her.

Unfortunately, when she left home later that year, the doll had to remain at home. She gave her prized possession to Ilse to look after.

3

Kristallnacht

On November 10, 1938, Ruth left for school by herself because her sister Hilde was recovering from a small surgical procedure. She didn't notice anything unusual as she made her way to school. When she got off the train and approached her school, however, she was astonished to see that it was in flames, as was the synagogue adjacent to it. The fire engines were just making their way to the fire, never mind that there was hardly anything left of the buildings. It must have been burning for hours (Figure 3-1).

Ruth was in shock. She didn't know what to do or where to turn. After regaining some composure, she decided to go to the home of the Rabbi who lived nearby, and rang his doorbell. The person who answered told her that the Rabbi and everyone were gone. She must have been the Rabbi's non-Jewish housekeeper, Ruth surmised later. The woman was amazed to see Ruth standing there with her school satchel and ushered her in to the house immediately. She asked why Ruth was there, and inquired, "Hadn't she known what was happening?"

The young schoolgirl just stood there trying to make sense of what she had just witnessed. The housekeeper told her she should go directly home the way she had come, but first she insisted that Ruth contact a non-Jewish neighbor in her hometown to see if things were

Figure 3-1. Exterior view of the large synagogue in Oldenburg. (United States Holocaust Memorial Museum Photo Archives #1175948. Courtesy of Abraham Levi. Copyright of United States Holocaust Memorial Museum.)

all right at home. She told her that all the phone lines had been cut to the homes of Jewish residents. So, Ruth walked to a nearby phone booth and placed the call.

She called their non-Jewish next door neighbor and inquired, "Was everything all right at her home?" The woman replied, "Your mother is home," and hung up the phone.

Ruth cautiously made her way home hoping and praying that indeed everything was okay with her family. She said there were lots of Brown Shirts (SS Men/Nazi Military) on the train bragging about what they had done. They were so jubilant because they had broken the windows of all the Jewish businesses in town, looted those businesses, and dragged the men out of their stores to arrest them. They had set fire to the synagogue and any other identifiable Jewish buildings they recognized, like the school, and terrorized the Jewish community.

Ruth, naturally, tried to keep a low profile on the train. Frightened as she was of her ordeal, she just wanted to get home to her family

Figure 3-2. Ruth's home in Cloppenburg before Kristallnacht.

Figure 3-3. Picture of shops broken into and looted as a result of Kristallnacht on November 10, 1938 throughout Germany and passersby too busy to care. (Germany Federal Archives. File: Bundesarchiv Bild 146-1970-083-42, Magdeburg, zerstörtes jüdisches Geschäft. jpg, Wikimedia Commons.)

where she could share the events she had seen and reassure herself that *they* were all safe.

She hastily rode her bicycle home after arriving at the train station in Cloppenburg, and then began to notice that changes in her neighborhood had taken place as well. Her home stood in the center of town on the main street. When she arrived on her bicycle, she was confronted with many swastikas that had been painted on the outside of her beautiful English Tudor home (Figures 3-2 and 3-3). Then she realized that the house looked dark—all the shades had been drawn. This was highly unusual for an ordinary weekday morning.

She walked into her home and immediately the sounds of crying reached her ears. Her sisters and her mother were in tears because the

Figure 3-4. Members of SA arrest Jewish men from Oldenburg, Germany and march them through the streets as bystanders look on. (United States Holocaust Memorial Museum Photo Archives #62167. Courtesy of Adolf Daniel de-Beer. Copyright of United States Holocaust Memorial.)

Gestapo (Nazis) had arrested her father and taken him with them. He was still in bed when they came to the door (it must have been shortly after she had left for school).

The Nazis hardly permitted him time to dress. "He left with his shoes in his hand," her mother said. Then, they shoved him into the back of their imposing black vehicle before allowing him time to put them on. He was 54 years of age, and not in the best of health. He had suffered a heart attack a few years previously.

All the Jewish men from approximately 17 years of age to the elderly were arrested that night and sent to camps for detainment (Figure 3-4).

The next day Selma heard from someone in Oldenburg that when they marched the Jewish men through the streets the previous evening, the observer had not seen Karl amongst them. This led Selma to believe that maybe he had been left behind in a hospital somewhere in the city. She sent Ruth back to Oldenburg to check the various hospitals to see if, indeed, her father might have been sent to one of them, but Ruth had no success in finding him. He was nowhere to be found.

She never saw her beloved father again!

4

The Kindertransport

Kristallnacht (the Night of Broken Glass) was the beginning of the end of the Simons family life as they had known it. Their Cloppenburg synagogue had been burnt to the ground, as well as over 250 other synagogues throughout Germany. They could no longer purchase kosher food and their bank accounts had been frozen by the government. Their dear next door neighbor told Selma, confidentially, that she would lend them some money for the time being if she needed it. The greatest impact on the family, by far, was that their beloved father had been arrested by the Nazis, and their mother was left to make life-altering decisions on her own. However... somehow, some way, and it is still unknown to this day, Karl found a way to send a note to Selma after his arrest. It is believed to have said, "Send the children on vacation," or something to that effect.

Ruth's mother was determined to save her family from the Nazis. She had hoped that the entire family would be able to emigrate together to America. Their immigration papers were applied for, but as everyone else was told, they would have to wait for their quota number to come up before they could depart.

Following the news of the arrest and incarceration of most Jewish men throughout Germany, and the destruction that took place on Kristallnacht, people in other nations began to take notice. "Some men and women of vision in Britain set out to persuade their Government to allow more persecuted Jews from Germany and other Nazi occupied territories into Britain. They met with little success."[1]

"The British Prime Minister, Neville Chamberlain, who had signed off on the Munich Treaty* with Germany and France, wanted 'no more wailing Jews'. Then on November 21, 1938, just eleven days after Kristallnacht, representatives of CBF, now World Jewish Relief, had a meeting with a gentleman serving as the Home Secretary of the House of Commons. Sir Samuel Hoare, was approached to impress upon him the seriousness of the situation and convince him of his obligation to help."[1]

Munich Treaty—On March 15, 1938 the annexation of Austria took place under the threat of invasion from Germany. It was called the Anshluss. Hitler was enormously pleased with himself that he was able to take Austria, his homeland, under his auspices.

"On September 28 and 29, 1938, the leaders of Great Britain, France, and Italy met with Hitler at Munich to resolve the political status of Sudenten Germans.[2] (Three million ethnic Germans lived in the Czechoslovak region of the Sudentenland and Hitler wanted them to be declared "autonomous" from the Czech government). When his demands were rejected, "Hitler threatened an invasion, thus precipitating an international crisis." "No Czechoslovakian leaders were allowed to participate in the conference."[2]

"The British and French, who had treaty obligations to support Czechoslovakia in the event of an attack were terrified that Hitler might invade, which would draw them into the war."[2]

In other words, the French and British looked the other way and gave in to the Germans' demands—instead of honoring their original agreement to back the Czech government in case they were in trouble.

"That evening, in the House of Common, Labour MP Noel Baker made an impassioned speech about the plight of Jews in German occupied lands."[1] Much debate and discussion ensued. The outcome resulted in Sir Hoare declaring, "that unaccompanied Jewish children of Germany and other children threatened by Germany would be allowed to emigrate to Britain without special visas. No limit was stipulated on the number of children that could be helped at that time."[1]

Initially known as the Movement for the Care of Children from Germany, it would become known as the Kindertransport. Kinder is the German word for children. "In total, nearly 10,000 children from Austria, Germany, Czechoslovakia, and Poland"[3] were saved by Britain's magnanimous gesture.

The Rabbi's wife in Oldenburg heard about the program that was established in England almost immediately. She told Selma and the other parents of the Jewish children attending the school who to contact to enroll their children in the program. Selma, left alone with the girls after Karl's arrest, was forced to make the agonizing decision by herself. She could only choose two of her four children!

She ultimately chose Ruth and Hilde. By then Ruth was nearly 14, and Hilde was 12 1/2, and she prayed that together they would be mature enough to meet and surmount the challenges these circumstances would present.

The middle daughters were hastily prepared for their trip. Then, Selma took the girls to Oldenburg and let them take the train to Hamburg to receive instructions and orientation for their impending journey to Great Britain.

Edith met her middle sisters a few days later in Hamburg and accompanied them on the train for a short while until her stop was reached, and she had to disembark. Ruth and Hilde hugged Edith for dear life. They weren't sure if they would ever see her or any of the rest of their family ever again. As it turned out, some of their worst fears would be realized a few short years later.

The two sisters each carried their own small suitcase filled with their basic needs. The girls' Kindertransport left on December 1, 1938. They boarded one of the first of many such transports that left Germany, Austria, Czechoslovakia, and Poland bound for English shores (Figure 4-1). On the girls' train there were children ages 4 to 17.

Figure 4-1. Ruth Simon on left of unidentified child and Hilde Simon on right. (Jewish Refugees who are members of the first Kindertransport from Germany arrive in Harwich, England. Photo Archive #1032503. Courtesy of The David M. Rubenstein National Institute of Holocaust Documentation. United States Holocaust Memorial Museum—Photo Archive #02725. Jewish Refugees: Search for Safe Havens [1933-1945]. Courtesy of Instytut Pamieci Narodowej and copyright of the United States Holocaust Memorial Museum.)

They each wore a number around their neck to identify them to the authorities as they traversed through their homeland onto Holland.

Their first stop was just across the Dutch border. Singing and excitement ensued once the children realized they were no longer in Nazi-occupied land. Once the train stopped at the station, there were hundreds of people lining the platform waiting to show their support to the children aboard. The crowd passed sandwiches and goodies through the open windows to the young passengers, along with notes of encouragement. The children were so appreciative. The crowd could only imagine what these Kinder had been through and the apprehension they were feeling.

Ruth and Hilde were grateful for the nourishment and their empathy. It was the most kindness they had been shown in a very long time. They had been taking turns crying on the train. They were so homesick and worried about their family. Where had their father been taken? Was he all right? What would happen to their mother and the sisters they left behind? Would they be safe in a strange country? They knew very little English.

Hilde recalls that Ruth would cry and she would console her, and then when Ruth stopped, Hilde would start crying and Ruth would console her. The train barreled on to Rotterdam, The Hook of Holland, that evening where the Kinder were boarded onto a ship to cross the English Channel.

It was a cold December evening and the crossing was rough. Even the sailors were getting seasick. Hilde heard one of the sailors say, after they arrived in England, that it had been the roughest crossing he could ever remember!

References

1. Green, Bea. Kindertransport 60 Anniversary Program. London: (Reunion of Kinder 15-17 June, 1999) Survival and Achievement, 1999:6.
2. Berenbaum, Michael. The World Must Know, 2nd edition. Washington, DC: The John Hopkins University Press, 2006:42.
3. https://encyclopedia.ushmm.org/content/en/article/kindertransport-1938-40

5

Life in England

The Kinder arrived in Dovercourt Bay the following morning. Dovercourt is a small seaside town in the county of Essex, England. Near there, in Harwich, was a summer camp that was improvised as temporary housing for the children (Figure 5-1).

The cabins were not heated and they were sparsely furnished. Hilde and Ruth were handed two blankets apiece and a wash bowl. There were two beds in each little hut. They were also provided with hot water bottles because it was freezing outside; the cold penetrated the flimsy walls of the cabins whenever the blistering December winds howled.

Many of the Kinder took ill between their weariness from the arduous trip, their constant fear and worry about their families and themselves, and the harsh weather conditions. Several of the Kinder caught Scarlet Fever and were sent to a hospital nearby. Both the girls caught colds and they were very homesick as well.

Still, they were well fed and tried to comfort each other as best they could. The sisters often thought about the home they had left behind and prayed for their family's safety. The Simon girls were only sure of one thing—by all means possible, they wanted to stay together. There were so many Kinder who had come by themselves;

Figure 5-1. Jewish refugee children from Germany, part of the children's transport (Kindertransport) were housed in Dovercourt Bay Camp after their arrival to the United Kingdom. (This picture depicts children enjoying the summer camp as it was intended to be; however, the Kinder arrived on December 2!) (Courtesy of The Institute of Contemporary History and Weiner Library. Holocaust Encyclopedia. Copyright of the United States Holocaust Memorial Museum.)

the sisters couldn't bear to be separated after all they had already been through.

The Kinder would arrive each week. The organizers would have to place them as quickly as possible to make room for the next train full. People would arrive daily from different parts of England to choose children to take back to their communities with them. Goodness was in the hearts of the majority of these individuals. Some truly became very fond of their charges, and considered them to be like "their own" after a time. Others took advantage of the children in various ways or used them as servants to compensate for the trouble and expenses they were incurring. The girls wanted to choose wisely so they could feel as safe and secure as possible. Their future could depend upon it!

A few days after the Simon sisters arrived, a group of Jewish philanthropists from Harrogate, Leeds in Yorkshire appeared at the Harwich camp. The committee was made up of several Jewish women and one Jewish gentleman. They were seeking to sponsor 25 to 30 religious girls to take back to their community.

Hilde and Ruth considered this to be a good omen. They had been raised religiously and felt that under this committee's criteria, it appeared that they would be honorable and trustworthy. And, as a bonus, by going with them, they would meet their number one objective, *staying together.*

They also had befriended some older girls in the camp that seemed nice and had good values, from what they could tell. Their new friends chose to go to Harrogate as well. So, they packed up their meager belongings and set off for their "new home".

It turned out to be the right decision for them. Harrogate was quite well known for its luxury spas and health facilities. Many wealthy English patrons would come to that region from all over England for rest and relaxation. It was a lovely, picturesque part of the English countryside, and the girls began to settle into their surroundings.

They were housed in a youth hostel and fed and cared for by the local Jewish community. Their housemother was a rather stern woman but they had come from a strict upbringing. They were required to keep their rooms in order and help out with some household chores, like setting the table and washing dishes. The girls wanted to do their part to get along with their new housemates, so they did as they were told.

As was required by their sponsors, they would pray before each meal and attend Shabbat services in the local synagogue. They dressed alike in their "sister" dresses from home and displayed good manners, so many of the congregants were fond of the two girls. Once in a while, after services were completed, they were invited back to one of the congregant's homes for lunch and dessert or treated to a movie.

Ruth and Hilde finally felt part of this newly formed household, and they made friends with the other young girls. They attended school Monday through Friday and were provided with extensive English lessons to help them acclimate to their new land.

The first Passover that the hostel was established was an interesting time for the German émigrés. The facility provided kosher food for its occupants, but it was determined that it would not be practical to go through the ritual of "koshering" the home for Passover. (That would require two separate sets of dishes and all the non-kosher for Passover food to be thrown away or placed somewhere for safe keeping during the eight-day festival). So, each child or several together were sent to congregants' homes for the week of Passover in order to observe the holiday properly.

In the case of Ruth and Hilde, they were chosen by their housemother to go to a Jewish boarding house in the area for the week. This was truly a treat for the girls. The wealthy boarders had come from various communities in England, and they were the only children on the premises. Again, the girls dressed in their "sister" outfits and were treated especially well by the guests. As a matter of fact, by the end of the week, each girl was handed several hundred pounds (English currency).

The girls were thrilled and thought they could start a bank account and save this money for their future. However, when they returned to the hostel, they were informed by the housemother that if they had received any money while they were "on vacation", that those donations needed to be handed over. Their housemother explained, in no uncertain terms, that the money was intended to support the entire hostel's expenses—not just the Simon girls!

The young ladies complied. They had had such fun on their adventure they really didn't mind, and were just glad to be back home. They all exchanged stories of where they had been, and it was wonderful to be amongst their friends again.

Naturally, Ruth and Hilde had been keeping in touch with their mother and sisters through correspondence, and had learned that their father had been released from prison. They were hopeful that they could all be reunited.

It was around that time that they received word from their parents and sisters that the rest of their family had purchased tickets to emigrate to Cuba on a boat called the MS St. Louis. The ship was due to leave in early May of 1939 from the port of Hamburg, Germany. Hilde and Ruth had hoped that the ship could make a stop in England so they could accompany their family. This would make all their hopes and prayers come true, and they could be one big, happy family again.

However, the ship was not able to stop in England on its way to Cuba. And, although the girls were disappointed, they hoped to leave England soon themselves to join the family in Cuba, or reunite with them in the United States once permission was granted from the U.S. authorities.

In December of 1939, Ruth took ill and, after several bouts of sore throats, she was sent to the hospital in Harrogate to undergo a tonsillectomy. It was around Christmas time, and the nurses "took a

Figure 5-2. Hiddy in England in 1939/40.   *Figure 5-3.* Ruth in England in 1939/40.

shine" to her. They kept her in the hospital for an extra few days so she could receive a special gift.

Princess Mary of Harrogate had been kind enough to drop some presents off for the children in the hospital during Christmas. She had asked the nurses in Ruth's ward to pick a young girl worthy of a little something "extra" in the spirit of the holidays. Ruth was the one they chose, and she received a lovely large, red and white gingham sewing basket filled with sewing supplies and thread. Ruth loved it, and treasured it for many years.

A few month's before Ruth's hospitalization, on September 3, 1939, Britain and France declared war on Germany after the Nazis invaded Poland on September 1. Approximately a year later, German bombs were dropped on London streets 57 consecutive nights. Other British cities incurred the German's wrath as well. In fact, Harrogate's own Majestic Hotel was bombed on September 12, 1940, but, fortunately, the girls' hostel was spared as it was located on the opposite side of the city.

Time passed. The girls grew up and they were now 18 and 17. It had been five years since they had arrived in England. The year was 1943. Their schooling was completed and it was time to go to work and support themselves.

Figure 5-4. The beauty shop in England where Hiddy worked.

While still living in the hostel, an apprenticeship was set up for each of the young women. Ruth studied her millinery (hat making) in a fine establishment in Harrogate, and also became a talented seamstress. Hilde learned her trade as a beautician (Figure 5-4). She worked in an exclusive hair salon in Harrogate as well. Hilde was quite adept and received extra training, which helped her establish her career when the pair finally arrived in New York a few years later.

Hilde and Ruth moved out of the hostel in Autumn of 1943 and acquired a roommate that Hilde had befriended, who happened to have a little boy. Their flatmate's husband, the father of the young child, had enlisted in the British Army to fight the war and received his orders to report elsewhere. The girls had their very own "flat", and they were pleased to be independent.

They continued to correspond with their family for a while, until the letters stopped coming!

6
Returning to Germany and the MS St. Louis

The Nazi government claimed that Kristallnacht, and the violence that they perpetuated, was payback for the criminal act that had been committed a few days before on November 7, 1938 in Paris, France. On that fateful afternoon, a young Jewish man of Polish descent named Herschel Grynszpan received a letter from his sister.

The letter detailed that Herschel's father, Zindel, and the rest of his family were deported back to Poland; even though by then, they had lived in Germany for many years. Hitler wanted Poland to take all the Polish Jews back, and Poland didn't want them back. Herschel's family was amongst 15,000 people that were shipped east for the purpose of expulsion in late October.

"The Polish patrol, acting on their orders from Warsaw, would not allow them to enter the country."[1] These victims of the Third Reich (i.e., Germany's government) were forced to wander in a wasteland of nothingness for several days, without provisions.

The weather was cold and damp and, finally, Poland relented and placed them in a displaced-persons camp within their borders.

After learning the fate of his family and so many others, Herschel became distraught, and then infuriated. He purchased a weapon and made his way to the German Embassy in Paris. The man he met with was First Secretary Ernst vom Rath. Herschel withdrew his gun and fired directly at him; vom Rath fell, and was seriously wounded.

The First Secretary was rushed to a Paris hospital, and for two days was in extremely critical condition. He succumbed to his wounds the evening of November 9, and was buried in Düsseldorf. "The incredible violence of the next forty-eight hours was described by the Nazi press as a spontaneous expression of public outrage over the death of Ernst vom Rath."[2]

There is no question, however, that this was merely a convenient excuse to unleash the violence and hatred that had been building up in Hitler and his Nazi followers for years. His unsuccessful Beer Hall Putsch against the Weimar Regime on November 8 to 9, 1923 had become a source of humiliation to him. That is when he and his Nazi cohorts were arrested in Munich by the police for leading a coalition attempting to overthrow the German government. The plotters had hoped to further their cause by marching on Berlin to launch a national revolution, but the insurrection did not come to pass.

Since that time, he had gained a strong foothold in the government, becoming Chancellor and then President of Germany, and in March of 1938 had successfully invaded his homeland of Austria. Each year since the installation of the Nazi regime, more and more Germans celebrated Hitler's triumph on that date. Yet, it must have irritated him to no end that he had been arrested and made to look foolish back in the earlier days of his illustrious aggressiveness for attention and power.

He was now the "Führer" of this powerful nation. This for him, was personal retribution! The dates of November 9 and 10, 1938 live in infamy for millions of people all around the world that perished or lost loved ones due to the insanity that was unleashed against the innocent on Kristallnacht and thereafter.

The Simon family would slowly be torn apart, starting with Karl's arrest on November 10. Unbeknownst to Ruth and Hilde, they would leave for England in a few short weeks. Left behind in Cloppenburg would be Selma, Edith, and Ilse, anxiously awaiting what they hoped would be the safe return of their dearly beloved husband and father.

Where Karl was during the immediate hours that followed his arrest is unclear. However, he was sent by rail on November 11 from

Oldenburg to Oranienburg, and imprisoned in the Concentration Camp called Sachsenhausen. Along with him, were over 900 other Jewish men (77 from Oldenburg and the surrounding countryside) between the ages of 14 and 82, who were also arrested during those harrowing hours of Kristallnacht. They were crowded into cattle cars for their ominous journey.

"The camp of Sachsenhausen had been built by Nazi engineers during the summer of 1936, just as the Nazi government was attempting to prove its legitimacy by hosting the Olympic Games in Berlin. It was located just outside of Oranienburg, a town twenty-five miles northwest of Berlin's Olympic Stadium."[3]

The prisoners arrived in the early evening and were forced to walk to their destination on foot through the light snow that enveloped them. It was cold and dark and the men were tired, hungry, and stiff. Rabbi Trepp, the Rabbi from the Oldenburg synagogue, was amongst the prisoners.

These Jewish men, now prisoners, drudged through the treacherous iron gates that proclaimed the all-together cynical motto of the camps: *Arbeit mach frei*, or "Work makes you free". "They lined up at attention in the Appellplatz", a roll-call area, located just inside the main entrance in front of the first barracks. They stood there all night long under "the threat of beating if they fell or if they had to urinate." "During the night more than a dozen older men dropped dead of exhaustion, cold, or shock."[4]

This was the orientation to which Karl and his innocent compatriots found themselves subjected. He was incarcerated for several weeks and then, as the majority of the prisoners were, Karl was released. However, before the prisoners were allowed to return home, they were admonished with a warning that might have made anyone's blood run cold: They and their families must leave Germany within six months time of their release from prison or risk permanent imprisonment, or worse!

Karl returned to his treasured family in Cloppenburg to learn that Selma had taken his note to heart. She had sent their middle daughters, Ruth and Hilde, to England on the Kindertransport. He must have been relieved, yet heartbroken, that he was unable to hug and say goodbye to them one last time.

The girls in England wrote on a regular basis and Selma made sure that their letters were acknowledged and responded to with lengthy letters of her own. She learned from their exchanges that her daughters were relatively happy, safe, and were receiving a good education.

Selma was relieved to report that their father had returned from his detainment. She didn't mention how tired and drawn he looked, or that he had dropped an excessive amount of weight. She wanted to keep the letters pleasant and relatively free of detail. Besides, she knew that correspondence from Germany to England was subjected to inspection. She wasn't sure who might read her missives between the time they were mailed and their arrival to their intended recipients.

Needless to say, Karl shared with his wife the dire warning he had received from his captors before he was sent home. Selma and Karl were both convinced that they had to use all means necessary to flee their *former precious* Deutschland, the country of their birth.

It was around that time that the Simons learned of a ship sanctioned by the German government that was to carry about 1,000 people, mostly Jewish refugees fleeing Germany, to Cuba. It was called the MS St. Louis. It was due to sail for Havana in early May of 1939, and the Simons, like so many other Jews, were hopeful that they could book passage on it to save the rest of their family.

The Simons had already applied for their immigration papers to the United States and thought if they could get to Cuba for the time being, they would wait there until their quota numbers were called. Besides, Karl's cousin, Julius Frank, his wife, Selma, and their young son, Gunther, had sailed to Cuba on a similar vessel some months earlier. They, too, had lived in Cloppenburg and they also had intended to wait in Havana until they were notified of their quota numbers having been approved by the United States.

Karl and Selma made the proper arrangements with the Cuban officials in Bremen, Germany, including purchasing special landing permits from a Cuban immigration officer named Director-General Manuel Benitez Gonzalez. "But Gonzalez was a notorious profiteer: he had amassed a fortune by using his position to issue overpriced travel documents to unsuspecting refugees. It turned out that those precious landing permits were invalidated a week before the ship even set sail, unbeknownst to those in possession of them."[5]

It seems that Gonzalez had been taking "bribes" for his personal gain for quite some time. Cuba's President Brú decided it had gone far enough and took Gonzalez to task for his greed. In turn, it was supposed to act as a warning to anyone else in the Cuban regime aspiring to profit illegitimately.

The Cuban government declared the certificates that the Director-General of Cuba had issued null and void, but it was kept from the passengers that had purchased them. These unsuspecting souls had been swindled not once, but twice!

In addition, it is strongly believed that Hitler was notified that these individuals would not be allowed to disembark when they reached Cuban shores. Hitler let the ship sail anyway. This would suit him just fine. After all, it seemed like no one wanted the Jews. If Cuba wouldn't take them and America wasn't ready to accept them, it would just prove his point—that Jews were a people of little worth to anyone. In other words, should he decide to pursue his ultimate plan of eradicating the Jews from Germany and other German occupied lands, who could blame him!

Incidentally, in addition to the passengers having to jump through many hoops to obtain their tickets, the voyagers were required to purchase a round-trip ticket. This must have made little sense to most of the passengers, but they were so anxious to escape from the clutches of the Third Reich, that they were willing to do whatever it took. None of them expected to *ever* see their homeland again, nor did they want to, given the dangerous situation in which they had found themselves.

A cargo ship containing some special possessions of the passengers booked on the MS St. Louis left Hamburg a couple weeks before their cruise departed. Selma, Karl, Edith, and Ilse carefully chose certain mementos and personal belongings that they did not want to leave behind and sent them ahead on that ship.

Amongst their cherished treasures were many photographs of their extended family reflecting memories of happier occasions throughout their lives. That freight was warehoused in Havana upon reaching the Caribbean island, with the expectation that the passengers could lay claim to it once they docked.

REFERENCES

1. Goldsmith, Martin. *The Inextinguishable Symphony*. New York: John Wiley & Sons, Inc., 2000:135.
2. Ibid., 136.
3. Ibid., 168-169.
4. Ibid., 169-170.
5. Sampson, Pamela. *No Reply: A Jewish Child Aboard the MS St. Louis and the Ordeal That Followed*. Pamela Sampson, 2017:24.

7
The Voyage and Despair of the MS St. Louis

The MS St. Louis set sail from Hamburg, Germany on Saturday, May 13, 1939, bound for Havana, Cuba (Figure 7-1). Aboard the ship were 937 passengers (930 of them were Jewish refugees). A large crew operated this burgeoning luxury ocean liner that was commanded by a German-born, Captain Gustav Schroeder. To say that the passengers were extremely fortunate to have such an honorable individual at the helm of their ship as their Captain, is understating the importance of the role he played in the events that transpired.

Captain Schroeder was a man of integrity and compassion. He told his crew, from the very start, that they were to treat these passengers as they would any other guests that they had served in the past. He was not about to let his patrons suffer any additional humiliation or disrespect once they were aboard *his* ship.

Of course, this was no ordinary cruise and these were no ordinary passengers either. The ship was required to fly the Nazi flag to identify itself. An image of Hitler was required to be displayed in the dining room on board the ship where the passengers dined. However, the portrait was covered up, by order of the Captain, each week when the Sabbath (Friday night) dinner was served. As Captain, Schroeder was hellbent on making sure his ship completed its mission. This

Figure 7-1. Postcard of the MS St. Louis. (United States Holocaust Memorial Museum Photo Archives #1109459. Courtesy of Gerri Felder. Copyright United States Holocaust Memorial Museum.)

included keeping his crew and passengers safe, and making sure they arrived at their intended destination on time.

The Captain was not made aware of the illegal status of the passengers' Cuban landing permits, even though the cruise line, Hamburg-America Line, was notified *before* the ship sailed! The company was now under Nazi jurisdiction, as were the railroads and all other major means of transportation in Germany and other Nazi occupied territories once the Third Reich came to power.

The ship was extremely large and magnificent. It weighed 16,732 tons and it boasted eight separate decks. It had graceful stairways and glittering chandeliers. A brochure that one of the Jewish passengers had picked up prior to his booking tickets for himself and his son stated, "The St. Louis is a ship on which one travels securely and lives in comfort. There is everything one can wish for that makes life on board a pleasure!"[1]

Note the picture of Selma and Karl boarding the ship on the gang-plank (Figure 7-2). Other photos depict Edith and Ilse on one of the decks of the MS St. Louis, and a picture of Karl and Selma enjoying a lovely meal (Figure 7-3). They look relieved and happy, perhaps even enjoying themselves a bit.

Figure 7-2. Karl and Selma boarding the gangplank of the ship MS St. Louis.

Figure 7-3. Selma and Karl Simon dining on the ship.

They must have felt that, at last, their family had made it to freedom. They were aboard this beautiful vessel sailing towards a new life. There had to have been many sighs of relief amongst the passengers because they had escaped Germany and were on their way to a country where they would be accepted as Jews. They were out of danger, and although it wouldn't be easy, this voyage had rescued them from the grips of evil, and quite assuredly had saved their lives.

According to Edith, who was nearly 17 at the time she boarded, she and Ilse (age 11) had a lot of fun. In Edith's words, "We were a group of young people who really had a nice time together." She recalled meeting many new people on board. There were parties every night for the young passengers. They were very grateful to finally be free of the restrictions they had lived under since the Nazis took control.

Edie (as she was referred to by then) even had a brief shipboard romance with a boy named Fritz. She remarked that there had been several other young shipboard romances that flourished amongst her teenage companions. She told a reporter from *The Palm Beach Post* many years later that, "It was nice, I got to go on a real cruise."

The ship was equipped with a small swimming pool, a cinema, and even had a swing band that performed regularly in the ballroom. The outside air was cold but fresh, and the open seascape was breathtaking. The sun shone on the comfortable deck chairs, as bundled voyagers ventured out wrapped in woolen blankets and warm outerwear. Once the ship was underway, tensions began to ease for some passengers (Figure 7-4).

On May 27, the ship arrived on Cuban shores. Everyone was anxious to disembark. They'd had their baggage ready for days. A horn alerted them before dawn so they could enjoy a hearty breakfast before they left the ship. Excitement was the order of the day. The passengers waited for several hours for instructions to exit the ship. It was hot in the tropical climate, but they tried to be patient.

As time went on, some of the passengers began to wonder what was taking so long to go ashore. It was rumored that there had been problems with some of the passengers' documents.

Little vessels, like rowboats, started appearing in the water surrounding the tremendous MS St. Louis. Their occupants were mostly relatives of people on board, already living in Cuba, coming to greet their long lost relatives. In one of those boats were Julius and Selma Frank, Karl's cousin and his wife, peering at the ship and waving to the crowd. Edie and Ilse spotted them and were so happy to see their familiar, loving faces. Words of encouragement fell on the passengers' ears. "We will see you soon." "Don't give up!"[2]

Then came orders from the Cuban officials at the harbor, that the ship was not to dock. The ship was forced to drop anchor in the middle of the harbor.

It turned out that "Captain Schroeder had received a cable from the home office in Germany on May 23, saying that the St. Louis

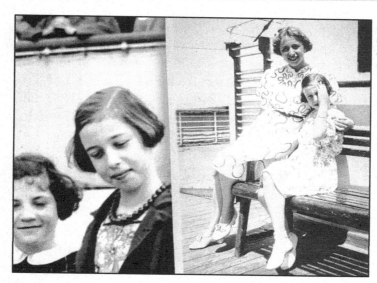

Figure 7-4. Edith and Ilse Simon on the deck of the ship.

passengers were holding invalid permits and might not be able to disembark. Schroeder understood this meant trouble and immediately convened a small committee of passengers, confiding in them the possibility that Cuba might not let us in."[2]

About 30 passengers were eventually able to disembark and were sent ashore. They were obviously holding legitimate documents, unlike the vast majority of Jewish patrons, who had been swindled!

What happened then, was a myriad of urgent communication took place between the small passenger committee aboard the ship and officials in Havana, New York, and even Washington, D.C.

"The passenger committee sent an urgent cable to the Jewish Joint Relief Committee in Havana, which immediately notified its office in New York: the American Jewish Joint Distribution Committee, the largest Jewish aid agency in the world."[2]

"The Joint urgently dispatched two people, attorney Lawrence Berenson and Cecilia Razovsky, on May 29, to try to help the stranded passengers." It was like a "tug of war." There were several factors that affected the negotiations including "corruption in Cuba, an unwillingness of the U.S. to force Havana's hand, and agitation by fascist forces at work on the Caribbean Island."[2]

"The Cuban Nazi Party was granted official status just seven months before the St. Louis sailed."[3] They had created much in the way of prejudice against Jews amongst the local populace, and it was now more evident and pronounced than ever. The right-wing Cuban-owned newspapers published articles defaming Jews who they said would be arriving in the Caribbean port from Europe in the middle of May. The papers cautioned the locals that these immigrants were willing to work for less wages and could take jobs away from hardworking Cubans. In other words, "watch your backs!"

"Additionally, two other ships carrying Jewish refugees had arrived in Cuba within 24 hours of the St. Louis." This only fueled the fires of anti-Semitism and concern that more Jewish immigrants (who the newspaper claimed were Communist-sympathizers) would be a burden on the island's residents."[3]

The U.S. government didn't want to intervene in Cuban policy, although "they tried informally to nudge the Cubans toward a humanitarian solution and maintained behind-the-scenes contact with both Berenson and high level Cuban officials."[3]

"Frantic negotiations began June 1, when Berenson met with Cuban President Brú."[3] Then, Brú decided he would not meet on the subject unless the ship was removed from Cuban territorial waters. The ship was forced to raise its anchor and head slowly toward the Florida coast in the United States. "By this time, the St. Louis was front-page news across the United States."[3]

A Jewish passenger aboard was so distraught he cut his wrists and dove overboard into Cuban waters. He survived because he was picked up and taken to a Cuban hospital; his family was unable to join him.

What was ironic is that all the passengers aboard the ship had already applied and been granted permission to emigrate to the United States, once their quota numbers were eligible. They had been resigned to waiting in Cuba until that happened, but, it was clearly evident from Cuban reactions upon their arrival, that they were no longer welcome there.

The stranded Jewish refugees prayed that under the circumstances they'd be granted permission to go from Cuban shores straight to America before their designated quota numbers were called. They hoped that they might be granted asylum by the U.S., since they would be eventually going there anyway.

Captain Schroeder realized that going back to Germany would have been devastating for these decent, displaced people. "Undaunted, he did everything in his power to find us safe harbor," states Henry Gallant. Gallant was 10 years old at the time he was a passenger on the ship. Many years later he shared his story with a young woman named Pamela Sampson who wrote a book called, *No Reply: A Jewish Child Aboard the MS St. Louis and the Ordeal That Followed*, from which many of these passages are gleaned based on Henry's memories of the voyage and his life experience.[4]

"Anti-immigrant sentiment in America was very high. The U.S. State Department refused to take any steps to allow the St. Louis passengers into the country. The chief of the visa division, A.M. Warren, issued a decision that the refugees on board the MS St. Louis, 'must await their turns on the waiting list and then qualify for and obtain immigration visas before they could enter the United States.' "[4]

"On June 3, Berenson submitted an offer to Brú's negotiating team, which included a $50,000 bond guaranteeing that the passengers would not become dependent on Cuba for financial assistance. Brú made a counterproposal, raising the bond to $150,000 along with some other stipulations. However, the next day Berenson was stunned to learn that Brú's offer was in addition to a $500 cash bond for each passenger, meaning another $450,000 had to be raised ... The money was promised to Brú the next day, June 5. Brú announced that a 48-hour deadline had been set for negotiations to be completed."[5]

"But events overtook Berenson, who apparently had thought—and was gravely mistaken in doing so—that there was room for back-and-forth bargaining and that he could possibly drive the price down. On June 6, newspapers reported a statement by Cuban Secretary of the Treasury Joaquin Ochotorena to the effect that Brú's conditions for the landing of the St. Louis passengers had not been met and that they would not be permitted to enter Cuba."[5]

When the ship arrived off the coast of Florida, the passengers could see the lights of Miami. The Coast Guard prevented them from getting any closer than several miles from the Florida coastline.

Finally a desperate attempt was made to contact President Roosevelt. "Help them, Mr. President, the 900 passengers, of which more than 400 are women and children." The passengers waited,

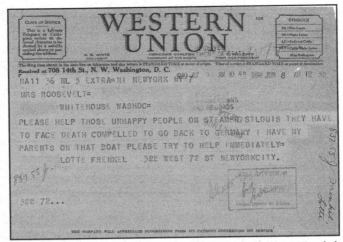

Figure 7-5. Telegram sent to Eleanor Roosevelt by Lotte Frenkel, whose parents were on the St. Louis. (ID: 799. Source: National Archives and Records Administration, College Park, MD. Creator: Lotte Frenkel. Date: June 8, 1939. Lights of Miami.)

but… "There was no reply. With public sentiment against immigrants, Roosevelt was not willing to run political risk for us," said Henry Gallant.[6]

An appeal was even made to Mrs. Roosevelt a few days later (Figure 7-5) by a child of a passenger on the ship, but there again, no response was received.

The Canadian government was lobbied by a group of influential citizens to intervene and accept the refugees aboard the St. Louis. They, too, refused. "Immigration Director Frederick Blair would go down somewhat infamously in history for proclaiming that no country 'could open its door wide enough to take in the hundreds of thousands of Jewish people who want to leave Europe; the line must be drawn somewhere.'"[7]

The ship was turned on its course back towards Europe. "Meetings were held instead of festivities, and progress in negotiations was relayed to the passengers."[7] Rumors were rampant and everyone was concerned as to what their future would look like?

What would become of these Jewish refugees? It seemed no one wanted them; the world had conspired against them. They were innocent, law-abiding citizens of a land they had been born into, and had lived and died there for hundreds of years. What would become of their precious children? Where was G'd?

REFERENCES

1. Goldsmith, Martin. *The Inextinguishable Symphony.* New York: John Wiley & Sons, Inc., 2000:214.
2. Sampson, Pamela. *No Reply: A Jewish Child Aboard the MS St. Louis and the Ordeal That Followed.* Pamela Sampson, 2017:25.
3. Ibid., 26.
4. Ibid., 27.
5. Ibid., 28.
6. Ibid., 29.
7. Ibid., 30.

8

What Happened to the Simons?

After the refugees were denied entry to Cuba, the United States, and Canada, appeals went out to many countries in Europe that they hoped would be sympathetic to their plight. "The Joint agreed to provide financial guarantees of support to any country willing to take the passengers."[1] Finally, the prewar governments of Belgium, Holland, France, and England agreed to take some of the passengers on board—if only on a temporary basis. The Netherlands took 181, France took 224, Belgium took 214, and Great Britain took 288 refugees.

Each family on the ship was given a questionnaire asking them their first and second choices, along with the request of any names of friends or relatives in any of those countries. Most passengers had wanted to go to England. It seemed the safest place of the four at the time, and for the Simons, they had two daughters there already. Their second choice was Holland—and that's where they ended up.

The ship made its way back to European shores and docked in the Dutch port of Flushing on June 17, 1939. Later that day it continued to Antwerp, Belgium. From these ports the passengers were dispersed to their "new" destinations. The passengers must have been so distraught by now and weary. What an emotional rollercoaster they'd been on. Most of them had used much of their resources just to pay for their passage on the ship. Imagine ending up back in Europe after all they had been through and yet, most of them were thanking G'd that they didn't have to go back to Germany!

The Simons arrived in Arnhem, Holland shortly after they disembarked the ship in Flushing. There they were met and were invited to stay with Karl's sister, Else, and her nineteen year old daughter, Betty. Else, as the reader may remember, was the sister who had introduced Karl and Selma to one another. She had grown up and married a man named Abraham Gerson of Bunde, Germany several years before.

Abraham had been a butcher there and made a good living. He died, unfortunately, in 1931 in Bunde, leaving Else and Betty to their own devices. Bunde was not a place that was known for its tolerance of Jews and Else and her daughter left shortly thereafter to be closer to family.

They initially moved to Quakenbruck to an Uncle and Aunt's house and then around 1938 relocated to Arnhem, Holland. They were living in Arnhem in the summer of 1939 when Karl, Selma, Edith, and Ilse arrived from their perilous journey.

On September 1, 1939, Hitler invaded Poland and the start of the war began. Then in May of 1940, the Nazis invaded the Netherlands.

It was shortly after the Simon family settled in Holland that Edie got the opportunity to leave for Coventry, England in August, 1939. She wrote to the family in Coventry that had offered her an opportunity to go to England to be their house daughter (before the ship the St. Louis left) and explained how the voyage was not successful. She told them how they were now in Holland and, if it was still all right with them, she would like to join them now. They agreed and she took one of the last children's transports (but not an official Kindertransport) to serve as their house daughter.

She lived with her "Coventry" family for nearly a year and half. Her documents came through in the Fall of 1940 and she traveled to Harrogate to visit her sisters before she departed for America (Figure 8-1).

She stayed for a week or ten days with them in their youth hostel. Ruth remembers the reunion was wonderful for all three of the girls. They were all concerned about the rest of their family, but seeing

Figure 8-1. The sisters finally reunite for a short time in Harrogate, England before Edie leaves for America in the fall of 1940. (l-r: Edie, Hilde, a friend, Ruth, a friend).

Figure 8-2. Ilse, Karl, and Selma Simon in the last picture taken of them in Arnhem, Holland in September of 1941.

Edie again was a dream come true. Before she left England, Edie promised to write to them and find a job so she could save money to send for them when their paper documents came through.

Meanwhile, back in Holland the family did what they could to survive (Figure 8-2). Food was in short supply and they didn't want to be a burden to the Gersons. Holland became slightly more anti-Semitic even before Hitler's invasion in May of 1940. Once Hitler gained control of the government, many of the same edicts were enacted that the family had been subjected to while in Germany.

Yet, they tried to make the best of things. Selma continued to write to the girls in England and this is a translation of the last letter that Ruth and Hilde received in 1943 before communication ceased:

> *Dear Children,*
>
> *It was a joy to receive greetings from you through a friend! We are here together with our relatives.*
>
> *We hope to remain together here! And always look forward to receiving news from you. We also received news from Edith that she is attending a bar mitzvah.*
>
> *On May 2nd, dear Hilde, you will celebrate your 17th birthday. Our good wishes are always with you both. Stay well and don't worry about us. Our dear G'd will watch over us always. Be strong and work efficiently. You are in touch with the Hermans (cousins of ours), Betty's mother in-law. Do you get together with young people your age? We have not heard from your grandmother.*
>
> *Be well and happy with love and best regards, Your parents*

Then Ilse wrote (she was 15 at the time)

> *My dear sisters. A thousand thanks for your writing to us. Send us a little picture of yourselves. I am as tall as mother. Best wishes for your birthday, Hilde. How many years are you in training? Greetings and kisses.*
>
> *Love, Ilse*

That was the last letter they ever received from their parents.

In December of 1942, Ilse and Selma, along with Betty and Else, were arrested and sent to Westerbork Transit Camp (Figure 8-3). Karl had been arrested earlier and sent there a few weeks before. They were there for a year and a half and then the family was dispersed.

Karl, Selma, and Ilse were sent on to Poland to Sobibor Concentration Camp on May 18, 1943 where they were gassed on May 21, 1943 (Figure 8-4).

Figure 8-3. Members of the Ordedienst, the Jewish Police in Westerbork, directing an arriving transport of Dutch Jews into the camp. (United States Holocaust Memorial Museum Photo Archives #24292. Courtesy of Trudi Gidan. Copyright United States Holocaust Memorial Museum.)

Figure 8-4. This is the site that Karl, Selma, and Ilse Simon were met with when they were sent by train to Sobibor Concentration Camp, from Westerbork Transit Camp, and murdered 3 days after their arrival on May 21, 1943. (View of Sobibor Concentration Camp I & II, Spring 1943. Courtesy of United States Holocaust Memorial Museum, gift of Bildungswerk Stanislaw-Hantz. Item #2020.8.1_001_ 010_0003. jp2)

Betty married a young man she met in Westerbork named Henry Herman on April 14, 1943, and they both survived the war at the camp.

Else was sent to Theresienstadt and then on to KZ Auschwitz. She died on October 11, 1944 from asphyxiation in the gas chambers.

REFERENCE

1. Sampson, Pamela. *No Reply: A Jewish Child Aboard the MS St. Louis and the Ordeal That Followed.* Pamela Sampson, 2017:30.

9

Edie Goes to America

Edie left England in November of 1940. Her documents had come through and she headed for the southeastern United States (Figure 9-1). Actually, she was fortunate enough to reunite with several members of her extended family when she arrived.

Her first destination was Jacksonville, FL. She went to live with an aunt, uncle, and two cousins that had come to the U.S. from Germany back in the mid-1930s. Tante (Aunt in German) Else (Katz) Meyerhoff (Selma's youngest sister) and Uncle Albert (Else's husband) had two children named Gertrude and Eric. Gertrude was 9 years of age and Eric was 6 when they arrived in the States.

Uncle Albert had had a brother who emigrated to America in the early 1930s, and had invited his brother, Albert, and his family to emigrate before things got worse in Germany. When the Meyerhoffs arrived in America, they initially worked in the orange groves and on a chicken farm in Fort Pierce, FL. They didn't know the language well, and tried to make a living as migrant workers.

As Gertrude and Eric grew older, Tante Else decided her children needed to be in a more Jewish environment so they could attend Hebrew school and make friends with other Jewish children. That's when they moved to Jacksonville and rented a house with many

Figure 9-1. Edith Simon's passport and papers.

rooms. Uncle Albert got a job as a porter in a local hotel. In addition to Albert's job, Else decided to rent rooms in their home to boarders to help with living expenses. Tante Else was a very fine cook and her guests raved about her meals. She gained a reputation for her business savvy as well. She eventually became the predominant kosher caterer in Jacksonville. She worked very hard, and she and Uncle Albert were successful because of it. They ran their business for 35 years!

Tante Else was also very active in the Conservative synagogue in Jacksonville and gave an impassioned speech to her congregation from the pulpit one day. Else explained that she had several young nieces and a nephew still in Europe, and was desperate to find sponsors for them so they might be permitted to come to the United States. She was not yet a citizen herself, so she could not sponsor them.

Some of the congregants agreed to come forward and help sponsor and save her sisters' children from the clutches of the Nazis. Edie, Ernest Ries, and eventually, Ruth and Hilde from England, were the children that all benefited from her zealousness. (More details of these sponsorships will be shared in the Epilogue).

Ernest was the only son of Else and Selma's sister, Helene (Katz) Ries; aka Tante Lene, as she was lovingly referred to by the Simon girls. Helene was sent to and imprisoned in Theresienstadt Concentration Camp in Germany in the late 1930s. Her husband, Arthur Ries, had been captured on Kristallnacht and subsequently was interred at KZ Auschwitz Concentration Camp. He died there when he was shot by a Nazi guard. Ernest was about 18 when his papers came through to emigrate to the United States from Germany. He, too, went to Jacksonville and lived with Tante Else and Uncle Albert. In addition, Uncle Meinhard, Else and Selma's younger brother, had recently arrived from Germany. Tante Else and Uncle Albert welcomed them all—it was a good thing they had rented a large home!

Edie stayed in Florida for one year where she helped Else run her business and then in 1941 she decided to move to Illinois to be with relatives of her father's. These were the Franks that had been in Cuba when the St. Louis tried to dock. They had left Cuba and settled in the Midwest of the United States. Their new home was on a farm in Forreston, IL, close to the bigger cities of Freeport and Rockford. Uncle Julius was also a cattle dealer, like Karl, the girls' father. Gunther, the Franks' son, was about ten years younger than Edie.

The girls were very fond of Uncle Julius and Tante Selma. Even though they were actually cousins of Karl's, they were older relatives (approximately the same age as Karl and Selma) and, therefore, referred to by the endearing term of Uncle and Tante. In Cloppenburg, where they had resided around the corner from the Simons, they had seen each other frequently and knew them better than most of the other members of their extended family. The older couple loved the girls and stepped into the role of guardians after the girls' parents and sister were killed.

Just to recap, by this time in the early 1940s Hilde and Ruth had graduated from their schooling in England. Initially, they were both set up with apprenticeships. Ruth learned to be a milliner (hat maker) and a seamstress, she worked in an upscale shop in Harrogate. Hilde went on to become a hairdresser.

Hilde worked in an extremely exclusive beauty salon in Harrogate, and proved to be very adept at her profession. She was taken "under the wing" of her employer and given special training. (The note that Ilse had sent her sisters, if the reader will recall from Chapter 8, had asked Hilde how long she was in training. The beautician training is what Ilse was referring to in that note.)

When Edie left Jacksonville and arrived in Forreston, IL, Uncle Julius and Tante Selma offered her the opportunity to attend beauty school to become a licensed beautician in America. Edie jumped at the chance, and after some training she began work in a local beauty shop in Freeport. She enjoyed her chosen profession and was able to save money, as she had promised, for her sisters' travel expenses when they left England.

Edie was a gorgeous, blonde, blue-eyed beauty, and she caught the attention of many gentlemen in that small community. She had a strong German accent, but her English had improved since she learned more in England, and then picked up additional proficiency when she arrived in America.

One night she decided to attend a USO (US Army) dance in Rockford. That night she met her future husband, Reuben Babich. Rube (pronounced Ruby) was a musician and served in the Army band. He played the saxophone, but was also a great pianist and a clarinet player. He happened to be off from the band that evening, but decided to attend the dance anyway and spotted a striking blonde girl on the crowded dance floor. He was American-born from Brooklyn, NY, and the son of two Russian-born Jewish immigrant parents.

He approached Edie, and asked her in Yiddish, "Are you a Jewish girl?" She nodded, and asked him in Yiddish, "Are you a Jewish boy?" And, he nodded. He told a reporter many years later that that was their first conversation. Then, they danced the rest of the night away...

Rube was only in Rockford for a relatively short time, but he promised to keep in touch with Edie, and told his mother back in Brooklyn that he thought he had met the girl he was going to marry. Esther Babich, Rube's mother, had some concerns about Edie after Rube described her. She didn't want her youngest son to have his heart broken. She thought Edie might be a German spy! So, Esther dispatched one of Rube's sisters to Illinois to "check her out". Edie proved to be who she claimed, much to Esther's relief, and Esther gave her blessings. Edie and Rube eventually got engaged, and were married in the summer of 1945.

Meanwhile, Rube shipped out overseas to London, and Edie asked him if he would mind trying to visit her two younger sisters in Harrogate. So, he made it his business to get to Harrogate on a weekend pass and brought Ruth and Hilde some chocolates and his K-rations (cans of food issued by the US Army to soldiers). These were often vegetables, fruit, and even meat that was rationed (scarce) in England during the war.

He even brought them some pairs of hose (before pantyhose), which were very hard to find during the war since they were made of silk or nylon and those materials were utilized primarily for parachutes for the war effort.

Needless to say, he was a big hit with the girls, and they were excited to meet the man that Edie was madly in love with for themselves. They gave him their "stamp of approval" and looked forward to joining their older sister and Rube in America soon.

10
Hilde and Ruth Leave England

So much had taken place since the girls arrived in England in December of 1938. They had found a home in Harrogate amongst other young girls their age and of similar circumstances. They had learned English and were receiving a good education in school as well as in Jewish studies. They kept in touch with their family as much as possible, and had learned through their mother from Tante Else that a Jewish family by the last name of Mizrachi was willing to sponsor the girls to come to the United States. Tante Else provided them with the address of these benevolent Jacksonville residents, and Ruth wrote to them. Here is a copy of the initial letter she sent:

(April 10, 1939)
Harrogate 10-4-39
Dear Mr. Mizrachi,

Just now we got a letter from our mother that you have given us an affidavit. You cannot imagine how happy we are.

We thank you very much for your generosity. We are now in England, with a troop of German Refugee children, in a Jewish home.

We are very satisfied here, but we hope to come soon to America so we can be together with our parents. We thank you once again.

Yours sincerely,
Ruth and Hilde Simon
The Jewish Convalescent Home
Harrogate, Yorkshire England

Then, in 1939, war broke out when Germany invaded Poland on September 1, and Great Britain and France declared war on Germany a few days later. Hilde and Ruth would not immigrate to America for another four and a half years, when their documents were in order and their quota numbers had been reached. In April 1943, a second letter was sent by Ruth to the Mizrachi's. However, she did not mention the possible reunification with her parents and youngest sister, Ilse. The girls had not heard from their family in a while and were afraid to project what their family's silence might signify.

The Jewish Refugee Hostel
Harrogate
10th of April, 1943

Dear Mr. and Mrs. Mizrachi,
It is such a long time since we last wrote to you that I am afraid that you might think we have forgotten you. But I want to assure you that this is not the case.

From our dear aunt we heard that you are keeping well, and we can say the same about ourselves.

We are happy here, at least as happy as we are expected to be under these circumstances.

We are both learning a useful trade and we are very keen on it. Hilde is a hairdresser and I am a milliner.

We are very much looking forward to the time we will be able to come to America. But I am afraid it will not be until this dreadful war is over. Hoping to hear from you sometime.

With many regards,
Yours sincerely,
Ruth and Hilde Simon

Once again, the girls had to rely on the kindness of others to bring about their dreams of leaving England and immigrating to America. But they were extremely grateful to these wonderful people who would help make it happen, and to Tante Else for her love and dedication, too.

By this time, Ruth and Hilde had completed their formal education, moved out of the hostel, and found a flat with a friend of Hilde's and her friend's young son. They were earning a decent living and supporting themselves. Things were different now somehow. Ruth was 18 and Hilde almost 17, and they had done all right for themselves considering, but they still longed to be with family.

The young women finally immigrated to the United States in December of 1944 (Figures 10-1 and 10-2). The war was still on, but their stars had finally aligned. They were aboard the Bayano (Figure 10-3), which was an armed merchant ship amongst a convoy of 14 others trying to cross "the pond" without incident during a World War! Twelve of the vessels made it to shore, while two were hit and sunk by German torpedoes. Their ship finally docked on Canadian shores in Halifax, Nova Scotia, on December 28, 1944. By then Ruth was 19 and Hilde 18. They had made it to North America!

From Halifax, they came through the state of Vermont to the United States and then took a train to New York City where they were met by their sister, Edie, and one of Rube's sisters. Edie was engaged by then to Rube, who was still serving overseas in the Army.

Mrs. Babich, an immigrant herself, was most kind and generous. She and Max, her husband, owned a coat factory. They supplied the young women with new coats, handbags, and other necessary essentials, and were extremely pleased to meet Edie's younger sisters.

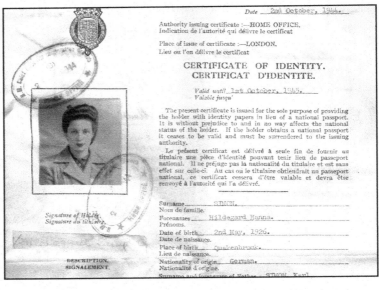

Figure 10-1.
Certificate of
Identity for
Hilde, 1944.

Figure 10-2. Certificate
of Identity for Ruth,
1944.

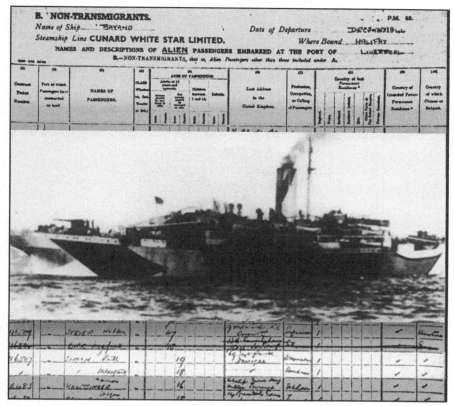

Figure 10-3. Ship crossing the Atlantic ocean in December 1944. Also depicted is the manifest from the Bayano including Ruth and Hilde Simon's name.

After a few days in Brooklyn, the three reunited Simon sisters traveled by train to Illinois where Hilde and Ruth were overjoyed to be amongst their dear Uncle Julius, Tante Selma, and cousin Gunther. Many hugs and kisses were exchanged upon their arrival, and the girls were truly relieved to have left Europe behind.

Hilde found work in the same shop that Edie was working in as a hairdresser, and Ruth went to work in a local dress shop as a salesperson.

When Rube came home from the Army in the Spring of 1945, Edie decided to move to Brooklyn, NY to prepare for their wedding. Hilde and Ruth came to the conclusion that they would join her. So, the former German Fräuleins, who had grown into young English ladies, were now living in America making decisions that would prove rewarding and exciting. For in Brooklyn, they would all meet their future husbands.

Hilde and Ruth found living quarters with a friend of Esther Babichs. In July of 1945, two months after the war ended in Europe, Edie became Mrs. Edith (Reuben) Babich, much to everyone's delight!!

*It has come to light that Edie wrote a letter to a friend in 1977 that was found amongst some other papers recently. The reader may enjoy the first-hand account of Edie's experiences that is included at the back of the book, entitled In Edie's Own Words.

11

Brides, Grooms, and Baby Booms

Once the girls were settled in their new place in Brooklyn, it was time for Ruth and Hilde to find paying jobs to support themselves in New York.

Hilde (who was now called Hiddy) took the glowing letter that her former employer had written about her from Harrogate and decided to "check out" a beauty shop she had heard of called Helena Rubinstein. It was quite well known and considered one of the most prestigious beauty salons in New York City at the time. It was located at 715 Fifth Avenue. Hiddy walked into the studio, looking very polished and professional, and shared her recommendation letter with one of the receptionists at the appointment desk. It seems that it warranted enough attention from a certain manager to come out from his office to meet her. Hiddy explained that after her experience in England she had worked in a shop in Illinois, and was prepared to start work immediately! Whomever it was she spoke to told her to come back the next day, and they would try her out.

Well, she went back the next day and worked on a few of their clients and no one ever told her not to come in the next day. So, as the positive person she always was, she showed up for work the next day, and the one after that, and so forth. At the end of the week, she got paid.

So, she had "made the grade" and was employed by one of the pre-eminent women's salons of all time. It was pretty impressive of her, everyone thought.

Now Ruth was not nearly as successful, unfortunately. She made the rounds of some of the stores in the city and then tried several factories that were pro-ducing women's hats. She found an opportunity in what she could only describe as a "sweat-shop" in lower Manhattan. She remembers being at her desk sometimes in the midst of sum-mer with no air conditioning and no open windows—and lit-erally having feathers fly up her nose from the fans that ran 24/7. It was not nearly as glamorous as her previous employment or Hiddy's, and the money was nothing to speak of either. However, both young women were able to pay their bills and that sustained them for the time being.

Figure 11-1. Edie and Rube Babich's wed-ding, 1945.

Within a few months after Edie and Rube's wedding (Figure 11-1), the young married couple found out they were expecting their first little one. Sandy (named after the girls' mother, Selma) was born in June of 1946. She, like her mother, was a gorgeous blue-eyed blond with lots of curls. Needless to say, it was a joyous event to welcome a new baby to their family (Figure 11-2). The blessing of new life made everyone smile.

Meanwhile, Ruth and Hiddy had heard about a Conservative synagogue that was in the Bedford-Stuyvesant section of Brooklyn that catered to German-Jewish immigrants. They decided to attend a service one Saturday morning to see if they could find some contem-poraries with whom to socialize. It turns out that during Shabbos ser-vices, they noticed a particular young man who kept staring at them.

Once the service was over he approached them and asked, "Are you the Simon girls from Cloppenburg?" It was so astounding to both

Figure 11-2. Edie and Sandy as a baby.

of them that someone would recognize them from so many years before, and they said, "Yes, we are."

The gentleman turned out to be Joseph Keller. He and his family had been attending the synagogue for sometime since they emigrated from Germany. This was the son of Max Keller who had stayed with the Simon family in Cloppenburg on occasion when their father, Karl, had sold them horses!

After a short while, they were all talking at once and were so excited to find out the Kellers had immigrated to America and were all right. Of course, the girls told Joseph about what they had been through and that they were not absolutely sure what had become of their parents or younger sister. Joseph was saddened to learn that news, but promised to tell his father all about them when he returned home later that day.

It seems that someone else was watching from afar in the synagogue that day as Joseph approached the young women. She knew Joseph and his father, and some time later inquired, "who were those beautiful young women to whom Joseph had been speaking?"

That older woman happened to be Johanna Gernsheimer. She and her family had emigrated from Germany some years earlier, and she had a son who was in the U.S. Army fighting in the Pacific. His name was Solly and he was in his mid-thirties and unmarried. After she got as much information about those young ladies as Joseph would share, she was inspired to see if one of them might just be right for her son!

Solly returned home from the Army the latter part of 1945, and his mother encouraged him to come to Brooklyn to attend the Chanukah dance at the synagogue. That night, Hiddy met Solly, and they were married the following March. Solly was living in a small town in Pennsylvania called Bernville. Two of his sisters and their husbands had moved there, and one of them had purchased a farm on which to raise cattle. Solly worked for his brother-in-law, and had bought a home of his own before he met Hiddy.

Figure 11-3. Solly and Hiddy Gernsheimer's wedding, 1946.

After the two were married (Figure 11-3), Hiddy, of course, moved to Pennsylvania… where later that year, she and Solly welcomed two new Gernsheimers to their family. Jakob Simon and Jeffry Charles were identical twin boys. They were the first boys born to the Simon family in a generation. So, two more bundles of joy arrived in 1946 and were added to the Simon family tree.

Ruth had to find a new place to live after Hiddy moved to Pennsylvania, and was able to board with a Jewish, German immigrant family she had met through the synagogue. They lived in Brooklyn with their only daughter, who happened to be about Ruth's age. Their name was Wallerstein and they welcomed Ruth to their home with open arms. She always felt like a second daughter to the warm couple.

Their daughter, Margo, and Ruth both attended services and were also part of an active youth group for single, German 20-year-olds. One spring evening, several of the members got together, and that evening is when Ruth met Manfred Heinemann. Fred was the current president of the youth group, and they shared a lot in common with one another. They seemed to hit it off pretty well from the start. Fred had been born in a small town in southern Germany in Bavaria, not too far from Munich.

He and his father, Sali, were arrested on Kristallnacht and sent to Dachau Concentration Camp for several weeks. Fred was only 16 when he and his father were incarcerated. He was one of the youngest prisoners the Nazis arrested that fateful night. He had been beaten

Figure 11-4. Fred in his Army uniform with his parents, Sabina and Sali, and his brother, Harry, circa 1944.

Figure 11-5. Ruth and Fred Heinemann's wedding, March 23, 1947.

up pretty badly by the Nazis and nearly starved, as most of the prisoners were. Fred was released a couple of weeks before his father. Within a few weeks after Sali's release, the family immigrated to the United States in December of 1938.

Fred had a younger brother named Harry who was 5 at the time. They all lived together in Brooklyn when they first arrived in the United States. Shortly after their arrival, Fred enlisted in the U.S. Army (Figure 11-4).

Ruth and Fred started seeing one another on a regular basis, and were married on March 23, 1947, at the same synagogue as Hiddy and Solly were wed (Figure 11-5). Ruth recalls that when they got married they had 35 cents between them, but they were happy and in love.

The year 1948 brought good news for the couple. They were expecting! When Ruth went into labor, she called her sister Hiddy and asked if she could possibly come to New York to help her for a few days when she got home from the hospital. In those days, when a woman gave birth, she was required to stay in the hospital several days afterwards—not like today!

Susan (also named for Selma) was born on September 12, 1948, and all was well with mother and child. Hiddy made arrangements for child-care for her twin sons, and made her way to Brooklyn to be with Ruth (Figure 11-6).

Figure 11-6. Hiddy with her sons Jeff and Jack at age 3 in 1949.

The day that Ruth and Susan were released from the hospital, Hiddy and Fred went to pick them up. Fred and Ruth lived on the second floor of an apartment building with no elevator. When they arrived at home, Fred helped Ruth gently up the stairs to their apartment while Hiddy stayed in the car with Susan. Then, when Fred returned to move and park the car, Hiddy proceeded to carry Susan to their second floor apartment.

She knocked on the door of the apartment she presumed was theirs and announced, "Here she is", and flung the door open only to find an elderly woman who was quite surprised at the visitors. The woman inquired who Hiddy was looking for, and she said her sister, Ruth Heinemann. The older woman explained that they lived down the hall, and after apologizing for the interruption, Hiddy and Susan made their way to the correct door, where they found Ruth anxiously awaiting their arrival.

Fred came shortly thereafter, and they all got a bit of a chuckle over the baby's surprise visit to their elderly neighbor. Thank goodness, the mistake was easily rectified!

12
The Definitive Letter

Nine months after Susan was born to Ruth and Fred, Karen was born to Edie and Rube (she was named after Karl). In the Jewish religion newborns are often named for beloved deceased relatives.

Of course, Edie, Ruth, and Hiddy had been very anxious about their parents and little sister's whereabouts since 1943 when the last communication was received from them. By now, they had almost accepted that their family had perished in the Holocaust, although miracles had been known to happen.

Rube was the one who pursued inquiries about his in-laws and sister-in-law, Ilse, in the hopes of finding out if they could have possibly survived.

In August of 1950, he contacted the Netherlands Red Cross once again, and finally in December Rube received his answer (Figure 12-1). The letter appears in part in this chapter. It was not what the former Simon women had hoped for, but it was closure for them at last. In their hearts, they mourned for their loved ones; it was a tragic end that none of them wanted to accept, but they still had each other, thank G'd!

The three sisters consoled one another in the only way they knew how. It seems that Ruth may have taken the news harder than her sisters. She had not even had the opportunity to say goodbye to her father before she left for England, and now he was gone.

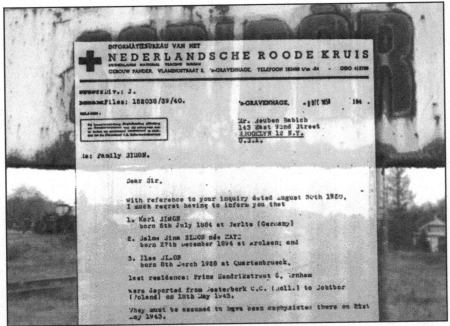

Figure 12-1. The letter Reuben Babich received from the Netherland Red Cross confirming the murders of Karl, Selma, and Ilse Simon on May 21, 1943 in Sobibor Concentration Camp by asphyxiation.

The finality of it brought Ruth to her first depressive episode. It may have triggered something in her that she knew her mother had also dealt with when the girls were younger. According to Ruth, her mother, as strong a woman as she was, had periodic mood swings and fought somewhat debilitating bouts of sadness. Depression can be hereditary and often appears/reappears in cases where traumatic events have taken place.

Fred was supportive and sympathetic to Ruth. He tried as hard as he could to show her compassion, love, and understanding, but he was still recovering from the dark side of things that he had experienced in the concentration camp. Susan was too young to understand the cloud that hung over her parents and tried in her own inimitable way to bring joy, laughter, and love to the both of them.

Fred and Ruth had opened a bakery for a short while after they were first married. The apartment above the bakery is the one that they had brought Susan home to when she was born (Figure 12-2). But, the bakery failed to produce a living wage. Ruth was no longer working because she was a stay-at-home mom, and Fred closed up

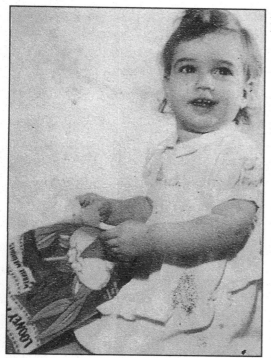

Figure 12-2. Susan Heinemann as a little girl.

the shop and found a job at another bakery. The hours were long and the work was hard, but Fred had a lot of talent. He had been trained in Germany as a pastry chef and reached the status of Konditor. He worked for a company called Kosher Bakers in Brooklyn and made wedding cakes, bar and bat mitzvah cakes, cheese cakes, and all kinds of fancy pastry for parties, caterers, and restaurants.

He sought extra training and was always reading. He joined the American Bakers Association and marveled at the photographs of the extraordinary cakes they displayed in their annual catalog. This was a science to him, and he worked incessantly on a notebook of his own design with hundreds of detailed recipes (tried and true).

Fred sought additional education by enrolling in Dale Carnegie classes in his spare time and reading voraciously. He thought about the future a great deal and decided that he would like to pursue a sales career in the baking industry.

In 1951, Hiddy and Edie both became pregnant again. Hiddy gave birth to Sharon (also named after Selma) in August, and Janice was born in October to Edie. Janice was named for Ilse ("J" being one of the closest letters of the alphabet to "I").

As time went on, Fred became anxious to spread his wings and put the knowledge he had acquired through his personal education courses to use. He began looking for new opportunities in sales and production in the baking industry on the East Coast.

In May of 1953, he was offered a position in bakery management in a company in Pittsburgh, PA. The couple decided that it was worth pursuing and moved temporarily to a boarding house in McKeesport, PA for the summer months so he could try out the position. As it turned out, Fred was not satisfied with the company, but landed another position with a baking supply company in Pittsburgh. He was groomed to be their new traveling sales representative in the New England territory and parts of Eastern Canada.

After some training about their baking products, Fred and his family moved back to their apartment in Brooklyn, and Fred started his new position. He was given a company car and traveled extensively Monday thru Friday just about every week.

In January of 1954, Ruth learned she was pregnant with their second child, and the baby would be due in early Fall—around Susan's 6th birthday. Susan was so excited about the baby and imagined being a big sister would be fun. They both missed Fred a great deal, but he was the family's only breadwinner and, after all, the family *was* growing. They both looked forward to his return each weekend, but he was often tired when he returned. Still, he made an extra effort to spend time with his girls. He missed them, too.

Fred was also financially helping out his parents and his younger brother, Harry. His folks had purchased a candy store/luncheonette/ice cream parlor in a rather rough section of Brooklyn, and it wasn't doing well. His brother was in college now studying to be an engineer and had to keep his grades up, so he was not in a position to help support them. Fred felt a lot of pressure to succeed, and succeed he did!

The baby arrived on September 20, 1954. However, Fred was out of town when the baby was delivered, and something was terribly wrong with the child right from birth. He was a little boy and they named him Gary Phillip Heinemann. He did not cry when he was born and his head was misshapen. The doctor explained to Ruth, after the delivery, that some tests needed to be taken; she received that news by herself.

Fred and Ruth were very anxious about their son and it was one of the defining events of their lives. After some time, the doctor met with both of them and explained that Gary had been diagnosed as a Mongoloid. The doctor said it was a form of "retardation". Gary would be physically, emotionally, and mentally challenged his entire life. In those days, back in the 1950s, not much was known about the treatment of individuals with developmental issues; it was recommended by physicians that Gary be placed in a "special facility" for his own good. In later years his condition came be known as Down syndrome; but at the time, the words "retarded" and "Mongoloid" carried negative connotations and society looked down upon those stricken with these impairments.

Ruth was emotionally weary. She blamed herself for her son's condition, even though there was nothing that happened during the pregnancy that she had done wrong. After the trauma of her childhood, leaving her parents, and eventually losing them and her little sister, this was yet another emotional and very personal blow to her. It made her feel vulnerable and depressed, and she resented Fred for not having been with her during Gary's delivery.

Gary would need a lot of special care and Ruth wanted him to stay at home with their family so she could give him all the love and affection he deserved. But Fred was insistent that they should find a comfortable, safe place for Gary where he could receive the proper treatment he needed from a professional staff.

The gravity of the situation and their differences of opinion affected their relationship for many years. Ruth, reluctantly, gave way to Fred's strong objections to keeping Gary at home, but it drove a wedge between them that took years to overcome.

Meanwhile, Susan was very excited to have a new brother, but her parents didn't seem happy, so she was very confused. She had looked forward to having a sibling. She was lonely, and wanted to be a part of a family with brothers and sisters like her friends and cousins. When Gary was brought home for several weeks, there seemed to be a quiet tension in the house. It was then that Susan was told that there was something wrong with Gary, and he was going to be sent away to another home. It was briefly explained that he just required special attention that her parents could not provide, but that she and her parents would visit Gary on occasion.

This left Susan extremely hurt, angry, disappointed and anxious. How could they do this to her baby brother, she thought? She just didn't understand, at all!!

Figure 12-3. (l-r) Sharon Gernsheimer in Bernville, PA with her visiting cousins Karen, Sandy, and Janice Babich, circa 1955.

It seemed to her that her parents were very upset with each other, and so as not to cause them any more pain, she kept her questions to herself. But, it took its toll on her, too. She was only 6 years old and what was she supposed to do with the way *she* felt?

For years she doubted herself and rationalized that maybe something was wrong with her as well, but it might not be as severe as Gary's problems. She resolved to be the best little girl *ever,* so they wouldn't send her away, too! It was such an agonizing, hurtful time for the whole family and, to add to the frustration, no one talked about it. It felt like shame.

Ruth succumbed to a deep depression, and her siblings and their families suggested that they all go away for a little while together to help her regain her strength and spirit.

That's when a trip was planned to the country—the Catskills. It was a wonderful memory for Susan, as she had her cousins with her and she could pretend they were her siblings, too.

Fred continued to travel but thought about moving his family to a more central location in his New England territory so he could be home more frequently. After some investigation, they chose the community of Framingham, MA as their new home (17 miles west of Boston). They moved in August of 1955, August 19th to be exact. They left Brooklyn during a rainstorm, which turned into the *worst* hurricane New England had had to that date, ever!

The weather conditions changed so rapidly from bad to worse that they were forced to get off the road to find shelter. They had a car full of belongings and ended up in a makeshift shelter in Waterbury, CT at the YMCA. The roads were so flooded that they could proceed no further.

Figure 12-4. April 1959 in Boston Commons. Jeff, Sharon, and Jack Gernsheimer pose for the camera while visiting Aunt Ruth, Uncle Fred, and Susan in Massachusetts.

Luckily for the family, Fred was driving his company car with Pennsylvania license plates. There happened to be a volunteer who was working at the shelter that night that spotted the plates in the parking lot. He asked who it was that was there from Pennsylvania, as he himself had moved to Connecticut from Pennsylvania. Fred piped up that it was his car, and the man said, "Anyone from Pennsylvania would be welcome to stay at my home nearby." So the Heinemanns packed up their gear and followed the lovely man home. Of course, it was a surprise to his wife when they all trudged in, but she was a good sport about it and made them feel welcome.

Naturally, it was a big adjustment living in Framingham. Ruth was further away from her sisters and by then Gary had been placed in an institution in Staten Island, NY. Fred was still on the road a lot, but Susan adjusted to her new school and Ruth sewed curtains for their new garden apartment and made some friends amongst the neighbors.

Fred got involved in the Jewish War Veterans organization when he was home, and Ruth with the JWV Ladies' Auxiliary. They joined a Conservative synagogue close by and life went on.

They were able to visit Gary every few months, and Fred's folks were managing as best they could. Eventually, Fred and Ruth bought their first home in Framingham, and things settled down for a while for each of them (Figures 12-3 and 4).

13

A Very Pleasant Surprise

Ruth, Fred, and Susan continued to enjoy their new home, and around 1961 Ruth became pregnant. Joy returned to the household, but it was short lived as Ruth suffered a miscarriage early in the pregnancy.

Susan was growing up; she was now 13 1/2. One day in July, 1962 Ruth visited her doctor for a checkup. When she came home, she had some stunning news. She was 37 and pregnant, again!

Given her previous two pregnancies and her age, the family was excited but cautiously optimistic. As the pregnancy matured without incident, they were all becoming more hopeful and prayer and faith were incorporated into their silent daily routines.

On the evening of March 12, 1963 Ruth went into labor. She had carried it full term. Susan went to her friend Margie Goldman's house to spend the night—she was a sophomore in high school by then. The next morning, on March 13 about 7:30 am, the phone rang at Margie's house. It was Susan's father, Fred. The baby had just been born, and the first thing Susan asked was, "Is the baby healthy?" She had hoped for a little sister all along, but was so anxious to find out that the baby was all right, that she held her breath until her Dad answered, "Yes, the baby is healthy." Then, she asked, "Is it a boy or girl?" He declared, "It's a girl!!"

Well, there was *not* a happier teenager ever than Susan Heinemann at
that moment. She was overwhelmed
and overjoyed at the same time. She
and Margie got to stay home from
school that day, and she began to real-
ize a miracle had taken place!

When Susan visited her parents
later that evening in the hospital, she
witnessed the pride and relief beaming
on their faces holding their perfectly
healthy, normal newborn (Figure 13-
1). After the despair and heartbreak
they had experienced with Gary, it was
a beautiful sight to behold!

Figure 13-1. Ruth and Julie as a baby in 1963.

Her parents wanted to name the baby Carol, but Susan wanted to
choose her sister's name herself, and they agreed. She chose Julie. It
was a combination of Julie Andrews being popular at that time, and
the fact that this baby was a jewel—and she would be treasured. And,
that's how Julie Ann got her name!

Ruth gave her the Hebrew name of her late, beloved sister, Ilse.
She named her Ilse Elise. It was one of the happiest times of Ruth and
Fred's lives and Julie's birth made their entire family ecstatic!

14

Gary

Gary, Ruth, and Fred's mentally and physically challenged son, was growing up in Staten Island, NY at Willowbrook State School, a New York State-run institution. They were not able to see him as frequently as they would have liked now, given they had a young child, growing obligations, and resided in Massachusetts.

Ruth and Fred were in touch with the facility and would read progress reports about him. When they did travel to New York from time to time they would visit him, but were not allowed to go beyond the large visitation room where friends and family were permitted. It never occurred to them that he might be mistreated or abused. What they saw seemed to be a clean and well-run institution.

However, "In 1947, the complex, which was built and managed by the State of New York, opened with the intent of serving those with developmental handicaps, but the dark reality of the conditions in the facility were kept out of sight from the public. Enter Jane Kurtin, the first journalist to try and pull the veil off of Willowbrook in a print exposé for the Staten Island Advance. She was accompanied by then-unknown reporter Geraldo Rivera who took a WABC camera crew into Willowbrook at the invitation of a whistleblower, Dr. Michael Wilkins, who provided Rivera with a stolen key and helped him hop the fence. Wilkins was desperate to expose the plight within the institution that former U.S. Attorney General Robert F. Kennedy once called 'a snake pit' " (untappedcities. com/2021/06/22willowbrook-state-school.)

Many violations of abuse and neglect were discovered. The facility was grossly overcrowded, there was a ratio of about 50 patients to one caregiver, there was not adequate fresh air as the windows had been shuttered, and the residents were often left in soiled clothing.

In addition, overwhelming evidence was found that there was a group of doctors and medical staff conducting "medical research" that exposed these patients to Hepatitis. Patients were frequently injected with the disease to find out how it affected them. Of course, this went on unbeknownst to the families of their loved ones.

Needless to say, it came as a shock and was an extremely painful realization for the Heinemanns. They had entrusted their sweet, innocent son to the State of New York *(in America)* and look what they had done to him. Recent memories of **what the Germans had done to victims of the Holocaust** were brought to the forefront, again!

Ruth says that in her heart she felt pain, sadness, and sorrow for what Gary had endured. Fred was enraged by the treatment his son had been subjected to. It was hard for both of them to grapple with.

How to trust the State from that point on was very difficult for Ruth and Fred. The State of New York was sued and the patients and their families (plaintiffs) won. They did not receive any monetary compensation from the State, however, they got something much more valuable.

Following the decision, landmark legislation was passed by the Congress of the United States that required every state to follow. It would *legally change the way in which the handicapped and the mentally challenged were treated and provided for from that time on.* Eventually, these laws led to the enactment of the Americans with Disabilities Act.

These sweeping changes gave Ruth and Fred the confidence they needed to allow the State of New York to care for Gary. Furthermore, since Ruth and Fred were no longer living in the state themselves, Fred asked his brother, Harry, to become Gary's legal guardian, which he agreed to. Harry took this responsibility very seriously. He was a family

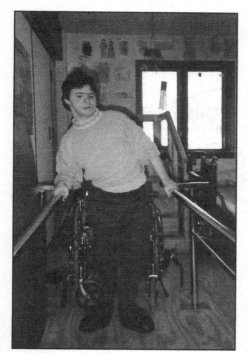

Figure 14-1. Eventually Gary learned to walk briefly with the help of parallel bars.

man by now. He had married a woman named Susan, who became the second Susan Heinemann in the family. They had a child of their own named Richard that was born six months before Julie. Both Harry and Susan had gone on to higher education and received their Masters' and then Ph.D.'s in Education. Fred was very proud of his brother, and trusted him implicitly.

Willowbrook State School was finally closed in 1987. By that time, all the patients that had been "treated" there were sent to facilities with satisfactory compliance to New York State guidelines of care.

Gary had been moved long before that to a facility in upstate New York and eventually one more time to a community home in Middleburg, NY, where he received very loving, superior care. He never did talk, he learned to walk very briefly with the help of parallel bars at the age of 39, but was mostly confined to a wheelchair (Figure 14-1).

He also learned to feed himself, however, he had become a Hepatitis carrier; perhaps from experiments that had been conducted on him or from exposure to other patients who had been used for experimental purposes.

Harry made sure from the moment that he became Gary's guardian that he kept in regular contact with the medical staff to which Gary was assigned. There were meetings and evaluations done on a consistent basis to which he was invited and frequent reports that specifically detailed every single physical, mental, and emotional condition that Gary exhibited.

Figure 14-2. Gary with Linda Klingbeil.

Ruth and Fred are very grateful to Harry and his family for their active participation in Gary's care when he was alive. In addition to the wonderful staff that Gary had from that point on, was a dear woman named, Linda Klingbeil, a social worker. She is still in touch with Ruth in 2022, as this book is being written.

Linda made sure to look after Gary with all her heart and soul. She was like a second mother to him and was as devoted to him as any mother would be (Figure 14-2).

Fred passed away in 2001. A few years later, Ruth and her entire family all traveled to Middleburg on Fred's birthday to visit Gary. It was the one and only time that Ruth had all three of her children together at once while visiting Gary. They took Gary out to eat and a picture was taken that afternoon that each of the participants will treasure for the rest of their lives (Figure 14-3).

Gary died in May of 2010 at the age of 55. He had been diagnosed with esophageal cancer. The family attended a very meaningful service in his memory in Middleburg, NY after his passing. In appreciation to those who cared for Gary, the Heinemann's had a beautiful patio and garden designed and constructed at Gary's day care facility. In addition to the flowers planted at the daycare that Gary had been treated in on a regular basis, a few flowering cherry trees were planted in the backyard of Gary's former residence, his community home.

Plaques were placed at each site with Gary's name on them along with expressions of gratitude to the staff. Harry was instrumental in overseeing the construction and planting at both facilities, and Ruth

Figure 14-3. The whole family at restaurant with Gary.

and her family are forever indebted to him for his devotion to Gary's well being.

One of Gary's caregivers wrote an ode to Gary and presented it to Ruth at the memorial service (see next page). It revealed a part of Gary that his family was not privy to, as they did not see him on a daily basis. This is what Gary taught them.

WHAT GARY TAUGHT US

Gary accepted everyone at face value. He didn't care how you styled your hair that day or that your lipstick was smudged. He didn't care what kind of car you drove or what type of house you lived in or how much money you had. He accepted us for who we were, no strings attached.

Gary taught us acceptance.

Gary loved to hang upside down in his chair and who knows what he saw that he wouldn't have seen from an upright position.

Gary taught us how to look at things from a different perspective.

Gary at times had to wait for things: the bus, his meals, his turn to be showered or changed, but he waited his turn and didn't complain as most of us do when we have to wait.

Gary taught us patience.

There were times when we told Gary "I'll get you some juice or a snack" and then something happened and we were later than expected with that juice or snack. Gary didn't hold that against us.

Gary taught us forgiveness.

And when we did arrive with the juice and snack, Gary gave us a big smile.

Gary taught us gratitude.

Gary accepted his illness and in his own way tackled it head on, going on when most of us would have given up the fight.

Gary taught us perseverance.

Gary faced many challenges in his lifetime, challenges that would leave most of us discouraged, disgruntled, and depressed. Not Gary, though.

Gary taught us courage.

Gary offered his hand to us, wanted to be our friend, wanted just to sit with us and spend time with us and share his life with us.

Gary taught us love.

15
Keeping Up With the Heinemanns

In 1966, Susan was 17 and a senior in high school, and Julie was 3. The girls' folks were helping research colleges for the fall semester for one daughter, while seeking a good preschool for the other. Susan selected Bryant College in Providence, RI, and their synagogue's preschool was chosen for Julie. They believed their son was being well cared for in New York at the time (Figure 15-1).

Ruth and Fred had both become quite active in the Jewish War Veterans group. Fred served as Commander of Post 157 for two years, and when he retired Ruth was elected President of the Ladies' Auxiliary. Then, Fred was nominated and won "The Man of the Year Award of 1967 of Framingham" for his participation and leadership in the community. He went on to be elected the National Historian of the Jewish War Veterans and win recognition for his superior scrapbooks (Figure 15-2).

As far as Fred's health went, he had developed high blood pressure and some other unusual symptoms. He was hospitalized locally at Framingham Union Hospital, but no conclusive clinical diagnosis was ever determined from the battery of tests they ran, so they discharged him.

In the meantime, he had been giving a lot of thought to his career and future goals. Fred concluded that it was time for him to make some professional changes in his life, which eventually led to his future success.

Fred created two new companies: Fred Heinemann & Company, an independent sales brokerage firm that represented several noncompetitive baking suppliers, and Tip Top Baking Company that carried bakery equipment (some that Fred had designed himself) and a line of wedding cake ornaments.

Figure 15-1. Formal picture of Fred, Ruth, Susan, and Julie in 1964.

Susan met Steve Berman from Monsey, NY at Bryant College in 1967. They graduated in 1968 and married each other, the love of their lives, in Framingham on June 8, 1969. A "special" wedding cake ornament from her Daddy graced their wedding cake (Figure 15-3)!

One of Fred Heinemann & Company's clients was a food flavor house from Elk Grove Village, IL, the Edlong Chemical Company (now known as Edlong).

Figure 15-2. Fred Heinemann, National Historian, hands a gift to an honored guest.

Figure 15-3. Steve and Susan Berman's wedding, June 1969. Shown above are Fred and Ruth; Steve and Susan; Susan and Harry Heinemann; Julie, flower girl; Sabina Heinemann, grandmother; and Richard Heinemann, ring bearer.

Their owners were impressed with Fred's salesmanship and made him an offer to move to Illinois and work for them exclusively as their National Sales Manager. In the summer of 1971, Fred, Ruth, and Julie moved to the Midwest.

They found a lovely home in Dundee, IL, where Julie enjoyed her elementary school and Ruth began to make new friends. They joined a Conservative synagogue in Elgin and became active there. Fred chanted from the Torah (Holy Scriptures) on Yom Kippur every year; he had a wonderful voice. Ruth took a part-time job in an art gallery every Sunday as both Fred and Julie had become Chicago Bears football fans and watched the games religiously. (One of the owners of Edlong was a former professional football player for "Da Bears" for a few years before starting the company, and there was a lot of talk about the games at the office on Monday mornings.)

Fred found himself going overseas to open up new markets for the company from time to time. He had traveled to South America and to Europe several times on business. In the summer of 1972, Fred asked Ruth and Julie to accompany him to Europe.

They all flew to Munich, West Germany in early summer and the city was teeming with excitement over the fact that they were hosting the Olympic games that year starting in August. After Germany, the Heinemanns traveled to London for the first time since the war took place. They also visited with a cousin of Ruth's in Manchester, England.

Unfortunately, a few weeks after the start of the Olympics, in September, the Munich Massacre occurred. This was an attack that took place by eight members of a Palestinian terrorist organization called Black September that infiltrated the Olympic Village, killed two members of the Israeli Olympic athletic team, and held nine other Israeli athletes hostage. Eventually, the remaining hostages were killed by the group as well.

When the Heinemanns returned from their European business/vacation they were stunned to watch on television the events that unfolded before their eyes in the very city in Germany that they had just visited. Needless to say, this heinous act was an atrocity and could have taken place anywhere, unfortunately, but it happened on German soil and to Jewish, Israeli athletes, to boot. It left another layer of anxiety to many—especially anyone who had been involved in the Holocaust.

In the fall of 1973, Ruth suffered a nervous breakdown. She was hospitalized for several weeks in Illinois, and recovered with the support of her family and professional help; her depression, once again, had re-emerged. Considering all she had been through, she realized that she needed to find a new purpose in life and concentrate on building her own self-esteem.

In 1974, while living in Wisconsin, Susan and Steve adopted a little boy and named him David Adam Berman. He was nearly 3 years of age, and his new Grandma Ruth, Grandpa Fred, and Aunt Julie were the first family members to meet him a few days after he arrived at his new home. Grandma Ruth had crocheted a vest for her new grandson and Grandpa and Julie enjoyed playing with him (Figure 15-4).

In May of 1975 Uncle Albert and Tante Else celebrated their 50th wedding anniversary in Jacksonville, FL (Figure 15-5).

David became a big brother when Daniel Isadore Berman was born to the family on July 4, 1975 in Williamsville, NY (outside Buffalo), where the Berman family had moved in December, 1974 (Figure 15-6).

Then, in 1977, Fred and Ruth were referred to the Mayo Clinic in Rochester, MN, because Fred was feeling very poorly and a CT scan of his head, at his local physician's suggestion, had revealed something significant. After many thorough tests, x-rays, and

Figure 15-4. Promoted to Grandma, Ruth meets David, her new grandson, for the first time.

Figure 15-5. Uncle Albert and Tante Else Meyerhoff, Tante Lene Ries, Tante Dora, and Uncle Meinhard Katz. (Else, Lene, and Meinhart were siblings of Ruth's mother, Selma.)

examinations, the Mayo doctors finally identified Fred's condition. He had developed a large tumor on his pituitary gland. From the size of the tumor, the doctors estimated that it had been growing for 15 years. Along the way, it had caused him serious hormonal imbalances, headaches, and significant blood pressure irregularities.

After his surgery, he felt like a new man. He had more energy, and he was able to function and

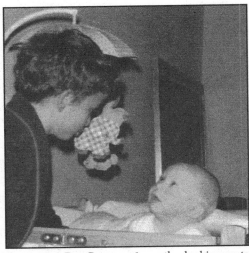

Figure 15-6. Dan Berman, 6 months, looking up to his big brother, David, age 4, in the winter of 1975.

think more clearly. He took up golf and joined some of his co-workers when they went fishing in Canada in the winter. He was like the *Six Million Dollar Man* (a show that was popular in the 1970s). Fred was promoted to Vice President of Sales and eventually to Executive Vice President of Sales for Edlong.

Ruth began to set new goals for herself and proceeded to return to school to get her GED (high school equivalency diploma). She excelled and graduated three weeks before Julie completed her high school education in June of 1981. Julie was 18 and Ruth was now 56!

Julie attended college in 1982 at Western Illinois University and then decided that she didn't enjoy it. She found a job in Illinois, and in 1984 moved to New York where she lived with her Uncle Harry and Aunt Susan Heinemann. After a brief job search, she secured a good one and started her new career with a consulting firm in Manhattan. Eventually, she moved to Queens, NY to her own apartment. After three years, Julie's bosses proposed that she join them as they were relocating their business to Raleigh, NC. She agreed to move.

Fred suffered his first stroke in the mountains of Arizona in 1984. Fortunately, Ruth had accompanied him on that trip. He had played a round of golf. His exhaustion, the elevation of the mountains, and his blood pressure—and the whirlpool he entered after playing—proved

Figure 15-7. Bar Mitzvah picture of David and family.

to be a dangerous combination. Ruth followed the ambulance in their rental car from the resort all the way down the winding mountains to the closest hospital in Flagstaff. After a few weeks of recovery, Fred's employer chartered a private air ambulance to fly them to the Mayo Clinic.

Ruth and Fred were in Minnesota for several weeks. He made a remarkable recovery and after some physical therapy was even able to drive again. In August of 1984 in Marietta, GA, their oldest grandson, David, became a Bar Mitzvah. Fred was well enough to travel and they attended the service and celebration (Figure 15-7).

Fred and Ruth had been married about 40 years when it occurred to them that they had a "bucket list" that they would like to accomplish. On this "bucket list" was a trip Ruth wanted to take back to Harrogate, England to visit the congregation that had been so instrumental in her and Hiddy's being taken care of during the war.

When they arrived, they met the gentleman that Ruth remembered as having been very active in the synagogue when she was a teenager. They asked him what he felt the synagogue would like, as they wanted to bestow a gift to show their appreciation. He suggested a curtain for the Ark (where the Torah is kept). They measured the Ark and ordered a special embroidered curtain from Israel for it. They

Figure 15-8. Karl Rosen in synagogue in Harrogate, England showing off the Ark curtain that Ruth, Fred and her sisters had donated.

also collaborated with Hiddy and Edie to compose an engraved plaque with words of thanks to the congregation for the support they had shown the Kinder during the war. The gentleman was very touched (Figure 15-8).

On another trip, Ruth and Fred flew to Israel and had an amazing time. It was a dream come true for them as they had been big supporters of many Jewish causes and had purchased Israeli bonds each year. They also visited Yad Vashem (Israel's Holocaust Museum).

By 1986, after his first stroke and the pituitary tumor, Fred decided it was time for him to retire. The company was reluctant to accept his resignation, but granted it. They offered him a generous retirement package and threw him a fabulous retirement party. Fred and Ruth began to spend the winter months in Boynton Beach, FL.

In 1987, Fred experienced headaches. He and Ruth returned to the Mayo Clinic, and this time the doctors discovered that he had a benign brain tumor called a meningioma. He was advised to watch it carefully, and if it started to interfere with his vision (having grown too large), surgery might be necessary to remove it. Eventually, Fred underwent Gamma Knife surgery (a very rare procedure at the time). The Mayo surgeons removed all they could of the tumor, but some still remained. He was given a regiment of drugs and warned that they might have some adverse side effects.

As it turned out, Fred's personality was affected by the drugs and what remained of the tumor. He seemed more high strung, more serious, and impatient. He had always loved to joke around before, but

Figure 15-9. Dan Berman's Bar Mitzvah in August 1988.

now he was less free-spirited and his temper was short. In time, he mellowed out some and was able to enjoy life's little pleasures once again.

Meanwhile, Julie met the man of her dreams on New Year's Eve of 1988 in Raleigh, NC at a party. His name was Richard Powsner. He had relocated shortly before they met in Raleigh from Long Island, New York!

In May of 1988, Ruth and her sister, Hiddy, traveled back to England. They visited London for the 50th anniversary of the Kindertransport. They recognized several Kinder from their childhood experiences.

In August of that year, Dan, the Heinemanns' younger grandson, became a Bar Mitzvah and the family enjoyed the celebration together (Figure 15-9). Then a few weeks later Susan, Julie and their parents traveled to Chicago to be at Richard Heinemann's (Harry and Susan's son) and Laura McClure's wedding on Labor Day weekend. It was a delightful summer of celebrations.

Retirement was agreeing with both of them and the warm weather in Florida during the winter didn't hurt either. They still lived in Illinois in the summer months.

After having become engaged in 1988, Julie and Rich tied the knot in September of 1989. They were a handsome couple, as seen in Figure 15-10.

Figure 15-10. Julie and Richard Powsner's wedding and family picture.

In 1993, Fred and Ruth moved to Boynton Beach, FL permanently. They had found a condo right along the Intracoastal Waterways and had a wonderful view of the boats as they passed by their enclosed patio.

The following year the family spent Thanksgiving in Raleigh at the Powsners. Susan and Steve came with their sons, and Fred and Ruth drove up from Florida. Rich's parents, Barbara and Norm Powsner, flew down from New York to celebrate the holiday with the family as well.

Fred was experiencing some health issues again. The family thought after a couple of good nights' sleep that he would feel better, and he did appear better when he awoke on Sunday morning. The girls' parents left to drive back to Florida in the early afternoon.

Then Julie's cell phone rang later that afternoon. It was Rich telling her that Ruth had just called. Fred had had another stroke while driving through Florence, SC on their way back. They stopped at a restaurant for a break and, fortunately, there was a nurse in the restaurant who came to his aid. They called the ambulance and he was transported to a Florence hospital.

Figure 15- 11. Fred and Ruth on one of their last vacations, in Vancouver.

Julie and Susan did not know what they would find when they arrived at the hospital several hours later. It was pouring rain, very dark
on the road, and they didn't exactly know where they were going. It
took them about 5 hours, but it felt like 20. They arrived at midnight!

They ran into the hospital and found their distraught mother who
said their father had been admitted. He appeared to be suffering from
slurred speech and his left side was immobile. It was several days before they felt he was out of danger. The girls stayed with their Mom
in a motel and eventually Fred was moved to a rehabilitation center.

It was a very stressful time for all of them. Eventually, the girls went
home to their families and Hiddy came to be with Ruth while Fred
recuperated. Fred was in rehab for about five weeks in Florence, and
Ruth never left his side. He was extremely fortunate; he was going to be
all right. When they returned to Florida, Fred had to undergo physical therapy. The stroke had slowed him down significantly. Eventually,
he made a good recovery, but was on a lot of medication from that
point on. That's when they decided that they wanted to take a trip with
Harry and Susan to Vancouver, Canada (Figure 15-11). In June of

1994, they traveled to Atlanta for a double mitzvah—Dan, their grandson, was graduating high school and Susan and Steve were celebrating their 25th wedding anniversary (Figure 15-12). It is one of their daughters' favorite pictures of the couple.

Figure 15-12. Ruth and Fred celebrating at the Berman's 25th anniversary party.

Fred and Ruth celebrated their 50th wedding anniversary in March of 1997. The whole family came to Boynton Beach to be with the happy couple and it was a wonderful family reunion and a beautiful party (Figure 15-13).

Later that year, in the summer of 1997 while watching television in their condo, Fred had his third and final stroke. It was a cerebral hemorrhage and it was a doozie! He had been taking a blood thinner and was monitored by his physician, but perhaps should have been monitored more closely.

Fred experienced severe repercussions and it left him compromised in many ways. Ruth had had some physical health issues herself, but took it upon herself to care for Fred at home for three whole years. She began to have bouts of various ailments in addition to fighting her constant depression and anxiety from the serious intensity of caregiving.

By the year 2000, it became evident that she could no longer physically or emotionally care for Fred at home. He was placed in a very nice nursing home and, by then, he was almost completely bedridden.

It was in early June of the following year that Ruth was hospitalized for some severe gastrointestinal conditions. Fred was reaching his final days on earth at the nursing facility. Susan and Julie went down to Florida to be with both of them.

Figure 15-13. Ruth and Fred's 50th wedding anniversary.

Even though Fred could no longer speak, Ruth wanted to say goodbye to him from her hospital bed. She asked Susan to hold the phone to her father's ear and Ruth lovingly told him that she forgave him for any hurt he had caused her, and asked for his forgiveness for anything that she had done that caused him pain during their 54 years of marriage. She told him she loved him very much and he acknowledged what she said by nodding to Susan, who informed her mother. It was very sad. That night, a few minutes before midnight, Julie and Susan received a call from the nursing home. It was their Dad's favorite caregiver, Jenny. She had been with him when he took his last breaths.

The girls arrived early at the hospital the next morning to see their mother, and as soon as Ruth saw them, she knew. She said she had experienced something miraculous the night before. She said she had been sitting up in her bed attached to her IV when she looked out the window of her hospital room to see, coming through the clouds, a young man dressed as a groom. It was a vision of Fred the day that they were married.

She laid back down on her bed and closed her eyes. She felt something warm on her lips like someone was kissing her, and when she finally opened her eyes, she said she felt like a bride. She got out of bed and proceeded to walk down the hall in her hospital gown pushing her IV stand, and a nurse stopped her. She told Ruth that she looked just like a bride! Ruth was released from the hospital the next day and Fred was buried two days later with full Military Honors.

Fred had had a hard life. He was beaten up during his arrest in Germany, on Kristallnacht—kicked in the head—which may have led to his many head injuries later in life. He worked hard and was a self-made man if ever there was one. He'd made a good living and was generous in his deeds, his time, and his donations. He had served his adopted country, America, proudly.

More importantly, he'd been a good son, a loving husband, and a great brother. He was also a wonderful grandfather and father-in-law. There is no question in his daughters' minds that he was, by far, the best father that any daughter could ever hope to have had; they attest to that to this day.

Fred died on June 25, 2001, just a few months before 9/11. His family is very grateful that he never knew what happened on that date!

16

Hiddy and Ruth Return to Cloppenburg

Ruth remained in Boynton Beach after Fred passed, and slowly recovered from her illness and the loss of her dear late husband. Most of the family had been with her for his funeral and the shiva (mourning period), but they had to return to their own lives and now she was on her own.

Edie, Ruth's older sister, and Rube had moved about an hour away from her to South Florida some years before. But unfortunately, Edie had contracted Parkinson's disease back in the 1990's and was growing weaker each day. Rube was a wonderful, supportive husband. It was a lot for him to take care of her, as he lovingly did; she needed a great deal of assistance.

Hiddy, Ruth's younger sister, had lost her wonderful husband, Solly, to a failing heart back in 1987. She still lived in Pennsylvania, and thank G'd was in relatively good health. Ruth and Hiddy spoke often.

Approximately ten years after Solly's passing, Hiddy was reunited with an old classmate from Oldenburg, Germany named Manfred Jakobs. They were married in 1999 and lived happily together until Fred's passing in 2006 (Figure 16-1).

Figure 16-1. Hilde and Fred's wedding.

Susan and Julie visited Ruth more frequently now, and Ruth kept herself busy by continuing her volunteer work at the hospital and going to Shabbat services regularly. She also crocheted and took some Jewish study classes. She thought she might want to become a Bat Mitzvah some day. In 2005 she did have a Bat Mitzvah. In fact, she had two. One took place in Boynton Beach at her synagogue and another in England a few years before with some of her fellow Kindertransport friends.

Edie sadly passed away in October of 2005. She was so beloved, but she had suffered so very much with her Parkinson's and the complications it had caused. It was hard to accept, but she was at peace and out of pain now. Her sisters envisioned her being embraced by their parents and Ilse when she arrived in heaven.

In August of 2007, Ruth visited the Bermans in Hamden, CT where they then resided. During her visit, they got together with a second cousin named Vera. Vera recounted the trip she had taken back to Germany with her siblings and her father, Michael, before he'd passed away. They had had an incredible time seeing his hometown through his eyes and learning new information about his past in the place where it had all begun.

Vera encouraged Ruth to consider returning to Cloppenburg with Susan. At first, Ruth resisted the idea, but Vera had been to Germany several times, and said she would go with them. "If Hiddy will go, so will I," replied Ruth. Hiddy agreed to go if her daughter, Sharon, would come along. Once everyone was on board, plans were made *(before anyone changed their mind)*.

On Friday, October 5, 2007 the two mothers and their daughters flew from Newark to Schiphol Airport in Amsterdam. After the seven and a half hour trip, they landed safely in the Netherlands and headed for their hotel. That weekend the four women did some sightseeing including visiting the Van Gogh and Rembrandt Museums and enjoyed a lovely ride down the main canal of the picturesque city.

Vera arrived the following Monday morning with a rental car. They decided they wanted to wait until they were all together to visit the Anne Frank Annex. It was an experience like no other; Anne and her family had hidden in that attic for two years, and what they had surmounted was beyond words. She and her family were discovered after someone unscrupulously disclosed their whereabouts. Anne's father was the only one to survive. Thank G'd she had left behind her diary containing the heartrending story of their ordeal. *Her diary should be required reading for everyone; there might be more understanding and humanity in this world, if it were!*

Needless to say, the group was eager to start their journey eastward. However, having been vividly reminded of why Ruth, Hiddy, and their family had left Germany (from their visit to the Annex), the participants were feeling somewhat anxious. The trip took about three hours through the city of Amsterdam, on to the modern highway systems, past many contemporary wind farms, and finally on to narrow tree-lined country roads.

They arrived at their charming inn located in Garrel, an adjacent town to Cloppenburg, and were relieved to have made good time. Hiddy and Solly had traveled to Cloppenburg some years before and had visited with former neighbors of the Simons—the Ruedings—and spent some precious time with Louie Averbach, their former Stableman, and his family.

Ruth had not been back to her *hometown* community in 69 years. It was an emotional journey for both Ruth and Hiddy and it brought up many feelings of angst, sentimentality, and sadness. The fact that they were with their daughters and cousin helped to comfort them.

After checking in and freshening up in the inn, they set off for Cloppenburg. Their first destination was to the City Hall, known as the Rathaus, where all documents were kept and business was conducted for the town. Ruth had wanted to see if she could get a copy of her and Edie's birth certificates. They had both been born at home and neither of them had official records of their birth. Ruth was pleased that she was able to secure those documents relatively easily. *The Germans always kept good records!*

There were two interesting things that caught the sisters' eyes at the Rathaus that afternoon. The first, was a

Figure 16-2. The Pingel-Anton bell.

large tabletop display with a small replica of one of Cloppenburg's old train stations and a train on tracks with surrounding landmarks just as it had been in the 1930's. This train and route Hiddy and Ruth recognized as the one that they had taken when they went to visit their Grandmother Ida Katz in Arolsen the summer of 1937. They also had the very bell that would be rung before each train departed. It is called the Pingel-Anton. This brought tears to their eyes (Figure 16-2).

The second point of interest was a poster pinned to the bulletin board in the entrance to the Rathaus. The poster informed them that a talk was scheduled to be given by a Jewish woman who had been a Holocaust survivor of Bergen-Belsen (concentration camp). The speaker was presenting her life story at an adult education facility *in Cloppenburg that very evening!* The Jewish, German woman had grown up in another German community and was now living in Israel. What are the odds of that happening on the day that these

Americans arrived? Ruth informed the group that she wanted to attend, and they all agreed.

The next stop on their itinerary was to the street on which their home had been when they were children. The address was 17 Ostrastrausse. The house was no longer there, but in its place was a home goods store with the same address. The street was still a main thoroughfare and looked very modern. The visitors walked up and down the avenue to get a sense of the town and its surroundings. It felt surreal to all of them.

It had been a very emotional day so far for the troupe. Hiddy declared, "I need a good cup of coffee and a piece of butter kuchen" (a delicate German pastry). They all exclaimed that that was a great idea, but they didn't know where to find a café? There didn't appear to be any on their street and they began to look around for someone to ask.

Suddenly, they spotted a nice looking elderly gentleman returning to his car parked near the sidewalk where they were standing. While he was unlocking his car door, Hiddy and Sharon approached him and called out. "Excuse me," Hiddy said, in German. The kindly man looked up and came over to her side. She began to explain in her seldom-used German that they were looking for a restaurant in which to have a cup of coffee. His English was almost non-existent, but he recognized that the group was not from the community. He asked her where they were from, and she told him, "America," and that they had just arrived. He asked what brought them to Cloppenburg, and Hiddy explained that she and her family had lived in the town before the war. Then he inquired, "What was your family's last name?" and, she said, "Simon" (pronounced Zeemoan in German). His face grew pale. "Not Karl Zeemoan!", he exclaimed. "Yes", she replied, "He was my father." The look on his face was incredulous.

He said, "I know Karl Zeemoan!" This man's father had been a farmer when he was a young lad, and his father had done business with Karl; he had purchased horses from the girls' father. The man said that his father was very fond of Karl and was so sad to see the family have to leave, especially under the harsh circumstances in which they were faced. Karl had left such a strong positive impression on this gentleman's father that to this day he felt the emotion. He told the women how well respected their father had been in his community.

Figure 16-3. Gottfried Bohmann and his newly found American friends: from left to right: Susan Berman, Sharon and Hiddy Gernsheimer, Gottfried, Ruth, and cousin Vera Wurst.

Sharon, Susan, and Vera were all surprised to hear what Hiddy was translating to them. It was as if the man had been planted there for them to find him on that *very afternoon.* He locked his car door and proceeded to guide the ladies to a local café for a "good cup of coffee and a delicious piece of butter kuchen" (Figure 16-3).

He told them that he wanted to show them something after they enjoyed their refreshments. He explained that the basement that remained after the local synagogue was destroyed was now Cloppenburg's hospital morgue, and that the Jewish cemetery was still there adjacent to it. He was insistent on showing them the plaque that had been hung on the side of the building next to the cemetery. It stated that this was the site of the former Cloppenburg synagogue and detailed what had happened there on Kristallnacht.

Gottfried Bohmann (his name) took them to the Jewish cemetery as well. There the sisters found many of the burial plots of their parents' former friends that had died before the war. They were all so enthralled by this captivating man who still had such a strong visceral attachment to their father through his own.

This was the first and only time Susan and Sharon had met anyone that knew their grandfather, besides their own family members. The women asked him if he and his wife would join them for dinner the following night at their hotel. Being a gentleman, he said he would check with his wife, but felt sure that she would agree.

There was another surprise awaiting Ruth, Susan, and Vera when they toured the cemetery. Hiddy and Sharon informed the others that Jack and Jeff (Hiddy's twin sons and Sharon's brothers) had been in touch with the town authorities before they had left on this pilgrimage, and had asked permission for the visitors to lay a stone in memory of their dear departed family members in the town's Jewish cemetery.

"The Boys" (as they were affectionately referred to by all) had even contacted a monument maker in Cloppenburg and helped design the layout of the inscription. The women were to go to the stone maker's shop to pick out a piece of granite so he could engrave the stone and have it ready to be laid and dedicated in the Jewish Cloppenburg cemetery before they were scheduled to leave on the following Saturday morning.

Ruth was very surprised by this revelation. She was so appreciative that Hiddy had taken the initiative to honor their parents and sister in this manner. Ruth had brought along the Siddur (prayer book) that had belonged to her mother. It had been one of the precious belongings that Selma, their mother, had sent ahead on the cargo boat that went to Cuba. It was one of the few treasured items saved by Uncle Julius and his wife when they retrieved the family's belongings.

The visitors' first day in Cloppenburg proceeded swiftly with all these miraculous, *beshert* (predestined) occurrences. Then, before they knew it, it was time to find the adult learning center to hear the Holocaust survivor speak.

There was a circle of chairs with a fair number of people already seated in anticipation when they arrived. Amongst the audience was a mixture of men and women of different age groups. It was evident that some press were also there to cover the event.

A gray-haired woman, about 80 years of age, appeared shortly thereafter and, in German, shared her story. She had come from Israel and was on a mission to speak to as many German communities in the area as were interested. Sharon, Susan, and Vera knew a little German, but it was hard to understand exactly what she was saying. However, from her facial expressions and the quiver in her voice, they could ascertain that it was painful for her. After the talk, a question and answer period took place.

Several people spoke up to ask questions and clarify some of her comments. Then, all of sudden, Hiddy was on her feet expressing her own thoughts. It was evident that she was a foreigner and people took notice of her comments, and then Ruth stood up and spoke as well. Ruth stated that she and Hiddy had been on the Kindertransport and were from Cloppenburg. It was such a spontaneous occurrence that the younger girls were quite astounded by the Simon sisters' sudden disclosures.

The woman who had shared her story was temporarily obscured as everyone started asking Ruth and Hiddy questions. No one's intent was to take any attention from the other woman. It was merely that the Simon sisters were from Cloppenburg and they appeared to be the first Jews to have ever returned to the community since the Holocaust.

They tried to excuse themselves as the press was asking more questions. Eventually, they all left, but their presence was noted. Several people asked where they were staying and how they could reach them for further discussions. They had all had a long, exhausting day and they were ready for a good night's rest.

From that moment on, they were like celebrities. A young woman that was attending the talk came over to them to inquire as to where they had lived in Cloppenburg. They shared their former address. She said that her father and his older sister, her late aunt, had lived on the same street in the 1930s. Her late aunt would have been a contemporary of their sister, Edie.

The next morning there were several messages for the Americans when they arrived at breakfast. The young woman named Anja Wienken, who they had met the night before, had left a message. Her father had found an album of pictures of his late sister and her friends, and she had identified some of the Simon girls in the pictures. Anja invited the ladies to come to her parents' tavern for coffee and cake and view the pictures they discovered of them as children.

Another gentleman had left a message. He was from the local newspaper, the *Münsterländische-Tageszeitung*, and wanted to interview and photograph the Simon sisters. And Gottfried had spoken with his wife and said they would be delighted to accept their invitation to dinner that evening. Later that day, an additional call was received from a woman who represented a Judeo-Christian group that wanted to interview the Simon girls on tape for two hours in order to share their answers with children in the community for educational purposes.

All these calls were returned, and everyone was accommodated. The reporter asked them to meet at the Jewish cemetery so he could take their pictures as they recognized some of its inhabitants. The very next morning there appeared a big article about the "girls" who had returned to their hometown (Figures 16-4A and B).

The visitors made their way back to Cloppenburg later that afternoon and drove to Anja's parents' tavern. Her parents were delighted to meet them; her sister was there as well. They were very gracious and shared delightful pastries and coffee while they passed around the album they had discovered for all to see. Yes, there was young Edie in some of the pictures, so recognizable, and Ruth and Hilde were in one or two themselves. It was amazing to the former Simon women to have found community connections still existed after so many years.

That evening Gottfried and his charming wife, Christa, came to the inn and they all had a scrumptious meal together. Christa was a delightful woman who was in the process of taking English lessons. They were an enchanting couple. Susan had asked Gottfried if there were any castles in the area, and he brought her a book filled with shloss' (that's castle in German). They weren't castles exactly, but large estates. Of course, the book was in German, but the pictures were self-explanatory. That was so thoughtful of him. He was retired now, but had been the Director of the hospital in Cloppenburg for many years. That hospital is where Ruth had had her appendix removed when she was around 10 years old.

The week went on and on with interviews and well wishers. The women also took some day trips. They wanted to see the graves of their grand and great grandparents, so they traveled to Wertle. There they were able to visit Simon Simon's grave and recognized several burial plots from other deceased family members.

On another day, they went to the community that Vera had previously been to with her late father, Michael, and saw the "Meyer"

MÜNSTERLÄNDISCHE TAGESZEITUNG   **OLDENBURGER MÜNSTERLAND**   DONNERS

In Cloppenburg beschließen Jüdinnen ihre Geschichte

Hilde und Ruth Simon gelangten 1938 in Sicherheit – Eltern und kleine Schwester im KZ Sobibor ermordet

■ Ihr Vater Karl Simon war Viehhändler in Cloppenburg. Erst nach der Pogromnacht 1938 beschloss er, die Familie ins Ausland zu schaffen.

Von Heinrich Kaiser

Cloppenburg – An einem kühlen, aber sonnigen Herbstvormittag findet die Amerikanerin Hilde Gernsheimer einen würdigen Ort, um ein dunkles Kapitel ihres bisherigen Lebens zu beschließen. Unter einer mächtigen Eiche stehen gut erhaltene Grabsteine, auf denen in hebräischer Schrift der verstorbenen jüdischen Bewohner Cloppenburgs gedacht wird. Namen stehen darauf, die Erinnerungen an Hildes Kindheit wecken. Die Willners zum Beispiel, eine hoch angesehene Kaufmannsfamilie, die in der Mühlenstraße ein Textilgeschäft betrieb. Oder Amelie Heiersberg, eine brillante Frau, die Hildes Schwester Ruth auf einem Sonntagsspaziergang in der Straße Hintern Wall versprach: „Du kannst alles schaffen, wenn du es wirklich willst." Efeu bedeckt die Gräber, und Hilde Gernsheimer freut sich, den Friedhof in einem so guten Zustand vorzufinden. Es ist ein guter Ort, um den Eltern endlich ein würdiges Andenken zu verschaffen.

Wäre die Geschichte anders verlaufen, wären Hildes jüdischen Eltern Karl und Selma Simon nicht im KZ Sachsenhausen ermordet worden. Sie wären vermutlich in Cloppenburg friedlich entschlafen und in einer würdigen Zeremonie an der Ritterstraße beerdigt worden. Aber es kam viel schlimmer, und jetzt wollen die beiden noch lebenden Töchter des Viehhändlers von der Osterstraße

Hilde Gernsheimer (rechts) und Ruth Heinemann, beide geborene Simon, gestern auf dem jüdischen Friedhof. Die Amerikanerinnen wollen in ihrer Geburtsstadt einen Gedenkstein für ihre ermordeten Eltern platzieren.   Foto: Th. Vorwerk

wenigstens einen Gedenkstein auf dem Friedhof enthüllen. Weil Karl Simon, der Jude aus Werlte, der sich 1912 in Cloppenburg niederließ, die Stadt so sehr geliebt hatte. Und weil sie selbst ihren inneren Frieden sucht. „Ich muss meine Geschichte zum Abschluss bringen", sagt sie, während sie mit der ein Jahr älteren Ruth den Friedhof nach einem guten Platz für den Stein absucht.

So lange er nur ein Stück trockenes Brot zu essen habe, wolle er Deutschland nicht verlassen, hatte Karl Simon sich und seiner Fa-

milie geschworen. Aber am 9. November 1938, der Reichspogromnacht, änderte sich seine Meinung abrupt: Der Kaufmann wurde in das Konzentrationslager Oranienburg-Sachsenhausen verschleppt. Aus dem Zug schrieb er seiner Frau Selma einen Brief: „Schicke die Kinder auf Reisen!" Ruth und Hildegard Simon waren damals zwölf und 13 Jahre alt. Sie gehörten zu den 9354 jüdischen Kindern, denen England nach der „Kristallnacht" Zuflucht gewährte. Nach Kriegsende wanderten beide nach Amerika aus. Auch der

älteren Schwester Edith gelang später die Flucht. Aber die jüngste Schwester Ilse und die Eltern schafften es nicht: Sie starben am 21. April 1945 in den Gaskammern des Konzentrationslagers Sobibor in Polen (siehe Hintergrund-Kasten).

Vor 27 Jahren hatte Hilde Gernsheimer schon einmal Cloppenburg besucht. Aber für Ruth Heinemann ist es nach 69 Jahren die erste Rückkehr in ihre Geburtsstadt. Es ist eine Rückkehr ohne Groll und Hass, aber mit dem Gefühl, noch etwas erledigen

zu müssen. „Ich werde bald 83 Jahre alt. Wenn ich es jetzt nicht mache, wann denn sonst?", sagt sie.

▼ In seinem Buch „Aus der Geschichte der jüdischen Gemeinde in Cloppenburg" hat Walter Demnis dem Schicksal der Familie Simon ein Kapitel gewidmet. Das Buch, das in der Blauen Reihe des Heimatbundes für das Oldenburger Münsterland erschien, ist in der Buchhandlung Terwelp in Cloppenburg und in der Geschäftsstelle des Heimatbundes, Museumstraße 25, erhältlich.

Figure 16-4A. Newspaper article reporting Ruth and Hiddy's return to Cloppenburg. (Reprinted from *Münsterländische-Tageszeitung.*)

family plots. They also met with an historian that Vera had located online who gave them additional information about the former Jewish communities in the area. He was very informative.

One night they had a magnificent dinner at Vera's favorite restaurant some distance away. It had been the home of a Baron at one time. There was an underground tunnel that led across the street to what was then a tavern. The whole place was so opulent; it was like a castle. The food was as fabulous as was the place in which it was served. Vera was a personal friend of the chef/owner, so he came out to talk with them and prepared a special dessert in their honor.

Each day was a new adventure. Another two articles appeared in the newspaper about the group during that week. Many people

Figure 16-4B. Newspaper article reporting Ruth and Hiddy's return to Cloppenburg. (Reprinted from *Münsterländische-Tageszeitung.*)

____ STADT CLOPPENBURG ____   MONTAG, 15. OKTOBER 2007

Im stillen Gebet gedachten Hilde Gernsheimer und Ruth Heinemann (Zweite und Dritte von rechts) zusammen mit Verwandten ihrer ermordeten Angehörigen. Ein Gedenkstein soll an Carl, Selma und Ilse Simon erinnern.   Fotos (3): H. Kaiser

Ein kleiner Stein als große Geste

Viele Cloppenburger wollten die Jüdinnen Ruth und Hildegard Simon wiedersehen

Von Hass war keine Spur. Die Jüdinnen äußerten sogar ihr Mitgefühl für das Leid der deutschen Kriegsgeneration.

Von Heinrich Kaiser

Cloppenburg – Es ist nur ein kleiner Stein mit wenigen eingemeißelten Worten, aber eine große Geste der Versöhnung: "Auch Sie haben schwere Zeiten durchgemacht, das wissen wir. Wir danken Ihnen, dass Sie gekommen sind, um unseren Eltern und unserer Schwester die Ehre zu erweisen", sagte die 81-jährige Hilde Gernsheimer am Samstag auf dem jüdischen Friedhof in Cloppenburg. Sie und ihre Schwester Ruth Heinemann waren aus den USA in ihre Geburtsstadt Cloppenburg gekommen, um 69 Jahre nach ihrer Flucht einen Gedenkstein für ihre ermordeten Angehörigen zu setzen.

Wie berichtet, kamen die jüdischen Kinder Ruth und Hildegard Simon 1939 zunächst nach England und später in die USA, wo sich schon die ältere Schwester Edith befand. Die Eltern Carl und Selma Simon und die jüngste Schwester Ilse wurden jedoch nach einer gescheiterten Flucht nach Kuba in Holland verhaftet und im KZ Sobibor ermordet.

Von Verbitterung oder gar Hass war keine Spur, als sich die Schwestern Ruth und Hilde einen lang gehegten Herzenswunsch erfüllten und in der Stadt, die ihre Eltern geliebt hatten, eine Gedenkstein zu platzieren. "Er soll an unsere Eltern und unsere Schwester erinnern. Er soll aber auch zur Menschlichkeit in aller Welt mahnen", sagte Hilde Gernsheimer.

Viele ältere Cloppenburger, die aus Pennsylvania und Florida angereisten Schwestern am Donnerstag in dem MT-Bericht wiedererkannt hatten, waren zu der kleinen Gedenkfeier gekommen. Sie wurde zu einer wahren Wiedersehensfeier nach vielen Jahrzehnten. Aber auch junge Nachkommen jüdischer Familien waren gekommen, um Ruth und Hilde Simon kennen zu lernen und ihnen alte Fotos zu zeigen. So brachte zum Beispiel eine junge Frau ein Foto von Peter Wiliner, einem Mitglied der Textilhändler-Familie aus der Mühlenstraße, mit. "Das war meine erste große Liebe. Ich war zehn Jahre alt", schwärmte Ruth Heinemann. Und Hilde Gernsheimer hielt ein

Alte Freundinnen und junge Cloppenburger tauschten Erinnerungen und Fotos mit den Schwestern aus.

Klassenfoto lauter bezopfter Mädchen in der Hand, das ihr eine ehemalige Spielkameradin mitgebracht hatte. Sie konnte kaum glauben, dass sie selbst darauf zu sehen war.

Wenige Stunden nach der Gedenkfeier verließen die Schwestern ihre Heimatstadt. Gestern traten sie die Rückreise nach Amerika an. Es war ein kurzer, aber intensiver Besuch zweier alter Damen, der tiefe Spuren in Cloppenburg hinterlassen hat.

recognized them as they went through the town. Ruth pointed out where a statue had been erected in the town square that had been there when she was a child. They also passed their former doctor's office. People gave them gifts and some of them were truly generous, and some were felt to have been given to them out of guilt.

On Friday night, they traveled to another community to attend a synagogue for Shabbat services. Ruth said it was an amazing experience praying in a synagogue in Germany after all those years. The president

Figure 16-5. Hilde and Ruth place the memorial tablet in Cloppenburg, Germany's Jewish Cemetery in remembrance of their dear, late parents and sister—Carl and Selma Simon and Ilse Simon.

of the synagogue was a distant relative of Vera's on her mother's side. (Vera's mother, Trudy, had also been on the Kindertransport, only she was from Vienna). The congregation was quite welcoming, and a certain satisfaction was felt by the participants from America—that they had all lived long enough to celebrate this milestone together. They said the Shehecheyanu prayer together (a prayer that expresses gratefulness, by the participants, to G'd for allowing this first time occasion to take place).

Saturday, Shabbat morning, the stone maker placed the beautiful inscribed tablet beneath the tree in the Cloppenburg Jewish Cemetery with Carl's, Selma's, and Ilse's name and dates of birth and death engraved on it (Figure 16-5). (Karl's name on the stone appears with the letter "C", this is the way it was spelled in Germany.)

It was a very moving ceremony. The air was crisp that morning, but not cold, the sun poured down from the sky and the mood was somber. There were about 30 people there, much to the visitors' surprise.

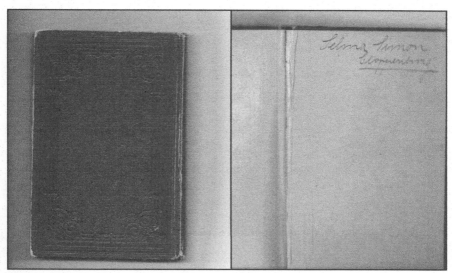

Figure 16-6. Prayer book and Selma Simon's signature.

There were officials from the town of Cloppenburg, and Anja, her sister, and their folks had come. Several members of the press were there. Gottfried and Christa Bohmann were there and many other dear people. It was an expression, the family felt, of a long overdue tribute to the former citizens of Cloppenburg who were violated and unjustifiably murdered.

The German/Hebrew Siddur with Selma Simon's self inscribed name above (Figure 16-6) was used in the ceremony to say Kaddish (the prayer for the dead) at the dedication to the memorial. The family chose to have the stone placed beneath a tree that appeared to have been about 150 years old.

Susan read a brief poem she had composed befitting the solemn occasion and then the Simon family left to travel back to Amsterdam and catch their flight back to America!

The journey had been a trip of a lifetime for these women. They had come to learn, to explore and to pay respect to their dearly departed family. They left with a sense of closure and a commitment to share their experience with the rest of their beloved family members as well as all future generations.

17

Returning to Germany as "Honored" Guests

Descendants of the former Simon family went back to Cloppenburg one more time in November of 2010. At the time, Ruth had been a bit under the weather, so she did not accompany them. Those that did make the journey were: Hiddy and her children, Jack, Jeff, and Sharon; Sharon's twin daughters, Carly and Julia, who were 15; and Susan and her two sons, David and Dan, in their 30s (Figure 17-1).

The town of Cloppenburg was celebrating its 550th anniversary the entire year, and they had invited Hiddy and Ruth to return, at the town's expense, to participate in the festivities as well as to attend a memorial event and commemoration in conjunction with Kristallnacht. The Town Council had also invited other Jewish families who had formerly lived in Cloppenburg before the war. Two other Jewish families chose to return as well—another family from the United States and a family that then resided in Italy.

The group left from Newark Airport and flew to Amsterdam where they stayed in the same hotel as the family had stayed three years prior. It felt like déjà vu for Hiddy, Sharon, and Susan. They were excited to share the unique canal ride. They visited museums and stores and enjoyed the fresh herring that was readily available. Jack and Jeff even arranged to meet a friend of theirs and her sister, who lived close by, to help show the group around personally.

Figure 17-1. The gang in Amsterdam (l to r) Susan Berman, Julia Levine, David Berman, Jack and Sharon Gernsheimer, Carly Levine, Jeff and Hiddy Gernsheimer, Laura Koenen (friend of the family), and Dan Berman.

The American visitors were made up of three generations now, which made the trip interesting in itself. They all visited the Anne Frank Annex together. Returning to the Annex took on a heightened significance for the ladies who had been there before, because now they were experiencing it through the innocent, youthful eyes of their children and grandchildren (Figure 17-2).

A few days in Amsterdam, and they were off in two rented vehicles to Cloppenburg. This time the group stayed in a very pleasant hotel in the town itself. Guess who was there to greet them shortly after they arrived—Gottfried and Christa Bohmann! The families had kept in touch with each other since the last time they had visited Germany. Their friendly, warm smiles made the town feel a bit more familiar to all of them.

A bus trip had been arranged by the town's welcoming committee to show their guests points of interest. The tour was given primarily in German, so not everyone understood it in its entirety, but it was a lovely ride in which the guests became better acquainted with their surroundings. A welcoming dinner was served when the bus arrived back at the hotel. It was a delicious banquet, and everyone met each other and enjoyed themselves.

Figure 17-2. Sharon and her daughters, Julia and Carly, with Dan in Amsterdam at the Anne Frank Statue near the Annex.

Figure 17-3. Susan with Hiddy, Christa, and Gottfried Bohmann at the Cloppenburg Reception.

The next day the Simon group wandered around town stopping in shops and visiting the street where "the girls" used to live. That evening there was a special reception and cocktail party and the Jewish families were "honored" guests. Hiddy was asked to say a few words as well as to introduce all of her accompanying family members, and she chose that opportunity to express her and Ruth's appreciation for having been invited. Several other speeches were made, predominantly in German. It was a nice evening and many of the townspeople introduced themselves to the visitors (Figure 17-3).

The following day was November 10—72 years to the date that Kristallnacht had taken place—and a significant ceremony was conducted. The town had engaged an artist named Gunter Demnig to place special markers called Stolpersteine (stumbling stones) (pronounced Stupelstein) in the ground in front of each of the sites of the town's former Jewish residences.

As one can see, each stone is affixed with a brass plate and represents an individual within that Jewish family. Each bears his or her name, the year they were born, and what happened to them when they were forced to involuntarily leave their home. None of the Stolpersteine could ever do justice to the fate these individuals were exposed to emotionally, mentally, or physically. But, this was a way in which to honor and memorialize these families having been citizens of Cloppenburg. It also serves as a visual reminder to all who pass the stones of the horror of the *Holocaust* and the *lives* that were taken and shattered as a result.

These Stolpersteine are being placed in front of homes throughout Germany and in some other countries "where there were other victims of the Nazi Regime such as Sinti and Roma, people from the political or religious resistance, victims of the 'euthanasia' murders, homosexuals, Jehovah's Witnesses, and for people who were persecuted for being declared to be 'asocial'. "[1]

As there had been nine Jewish families living in Cloppenburg in the 1930s, each of their former residences were visited. The invited guests and townspeople followed the town's spokesperson and organizers all morning and afternoon long, from place to place. While the custom stones were embedded, another group of individuals performed a song, read poetry, or shared a significant expression of the solemnity of the day. At the first former Jewish home visited, a local church choir sang several beautiful German hymns followed by the song, "We Shall Overcome" in English. That was quite meaningful, especially for the Americans.

At the Simons' former residence, there were a number of school-aged children from the parochial school that the Simon girls had attended before the law was passed prohibiting their attendance. The children read poems in German and in English that were appropriate for the occasion. It was quite touching. After the stones were laid at each location, several flowers were placed upon them (Figure 17-4).

Figure 17-4. Stolpersteine placed at former Simon residence.

At the former house of Tante Selma and Uncle Julius Frank, there was a band of children from another local school that played a cacophony of several different instruments. Each student played his or her own song, but all at once. The sound emitted was loud, chaotic, and out of sync—it was perfect for the purpose of a Kristallnacht memorial. It made the crowd feel desperate, scared, and wanting to escape. It evoked feelings that those who were being memorialized must have felt when they were experiencing those awful, hateful times (Figure 17-5).

The brutal cold from the damp, windy weather matched the crowd's raw emotions. Everyone was practically frozen stiff when they returned to the hotel for what they hoped would be a warm, hearty meal. The experiences of the day had been so emotional and exhausting. However, the dining room was closed when they arrived back at their hotel.

Anja, the young woman who had invited the former Simon girls previously to her parents' tavern, came to the rescue. She had been accompanying the visitors from home to home along with Christa and Gottfried to lend their moral support. After Anja realized everyone was starved and the dining room had already closed in the hotel, she thoughtfully contacted her parents, who graciously opened their tavern to the weary travelers.

Anja's mother whipped up some delicious fare and there was a warm, cozy fire in the hearth. Their American guests were so very

Figure 17-5. Sharon, Hiddy, Carly, Julia, Susan, and Jeff standing outside Uncle Julius and Tante Selma's former home in Cloppenburg, Germany.

appreciative for their generous hospitality and were finally able to relax a bit from the weary emotional and physical exhaustion they had experienced from the day's events.

That night was another special presentation. Each year, in the past several years, a local high school in the community had put on a play or performance to commemorate the horror and destruction that had taken place that evening on Kristallnacht, November 10, 1938. In 2010, the high school's presentation was most effective. It took place in a church across from the Jewish cemetery in Cloppenburg.

The church was quite full and, as the audience filed in and filled the sanctuary, this is what they saw before them. There was a stage with a podium to the left and a shelving unit next to that on which were placed cement blocks numbered one to ten. In the middle of the stage stood a portable movie screen with a light behind it. One could see two silhouettes standing behind the screen. One man was dressed in a suit or uniform of some sort and the other appeared to be dressed as a priest. A table stood to the right side of the stage.

The program began with a short introduction from one of the teachers, followed by a brief commentary (in German) by one of the students. Then the two men faced one another on opposite sides (but still behind the screen) leaving white space between them. They began to read from scripts one could see them holding. Occasionally, a degrading cartoon or a photograph of a German newspaper article would appear on the screen between them. From the dates on the borders of the newspapers, one could tell they were printed before and during the Holocaust.

The man dressed in the uniform represented the Nazi government, perhaps an official, who would read the headlines from the article displayed on the screen or make a declaration as if he were announcing a decree (a new discriminative law that had been enacted). The priest would respond in a voice of resignation, but also somewhat as a plea to the official. Then, another student would appear from beside the shelf and take one of the numbered blocks down and place it on the table adjacent to the screen.

At first it was not evident what was going on, especially since it was all done in German. But after a while, the audience began to see the correlation of the numbered blocks. Each block numbered from one to ten corresponded to one of the Ten Commandments.

For every freedom that was taken away from those persecuted, there was a corresponding commandment that was being broken. This is what the priest was conveying to the other man who just didn't seem to care or show any emotion whatsoever.

Finally, when the Nazis started murdering the Jews in gas chambers, the block with the Number 10 was removed from the shelf. This was the commandment, "Thou Shalt Not Murder". It, too, was placed on the table. It was placed on top of all the other blocks. Once the actions of the performers were revealed, the true significance of the presentation sent a strong message that transcended any language barrier. The actors conveyed the tension of their performances with few words but facial expressions and body blocking that made the audience feel as if they were witnessing these events in real time.

The play was followed by some songs. Everyone was given a candle and handed a small stone. All the participants and their guests lit their candles and walked a short distance to the Jewish cemetery across the way where prayers were read and each person placed their stone on a gravestone. (It is a Jewish tradition for a person when visiting a Jewish grave to place a stone on the plaque or monument of the deceased to signify their having been there to pay their respects).

Of course, those in the Simon family placed their stones on the memorial marker that had been dedicated to Karl, Selma, and Ilse the last time their family had visited Cloppenburg. Then, the candles were extinguished, just like the lives of the six million Jews and the millions of other individuals who were senselessly murdered.

Following the ceremony there was a reception in the rectory across from the church. The play had left a powerful impression on its audience and had demonstrated how very tragic this commemoration is considered by the German populace of today.

When asked, the Simon family participants felt moved by the impact of the entire emotional journey in which they had shared with one another. The young girls, in particular, were even more considerate of their dear grandmother, Hiddy, than usual, for they realized the pain of the past was being revisited by her. In their own way, each of the "Simons" were left to deal with the senseless tragedy that affected their family in Germany, Cuba, Holland, England, and Poland during the Holocaust. In total, they had lost 37 members of their immediate and extended family.

The following morning, the group said their farewells and returned to Amsterdam to board their plane. Ruth anxiously awaited the stories that were shared by her family. It was clear that new insight and appreciation had been gained toward those lost family members that had sacrificed so much so that the Simon family could prevail.

REFERENCE

1. (https://www.stolpersteine-berlin.de/en/node/1)

18

Ruth Learns to Fully Embrace Life

Ruth relocated from Boynton Beach, FL to Marietta, GA to be close to her elder daughter, Susan, and her husband, Steve, in 2017. She moved into an independent living unit of a senior housing complex and regularly attended services in a nearby synagogue.

At 93 years of age, Ruth joyfully traveled to the mountains of Callicoon, NY to witness the marriage of her youngest grandson, Dan, to a beautiful, sweet young woman, Betsy Steed, in September, 2018. She even helped sew the chuppah (wedding canopy) under which the couple spoke their wedding vows (Figures 18-1 through 3).

Hiddy, her lovely younger sister, unfortunately, passed away a few months later in March, 2019 when she suffered a debilitating stroke. She was nearly 92 years of age. The two sisters had been through so much together.

Ruth and the rest of her family attended a beautiful service in Reading, PA at Hiddy's synagogue. Over 300 people were in the sanctuary; it was standing room only. Several heartfelt tributes were shared honoring Hilde's life and warm spirit. She was so beloved and admired by her family and her community.

Things became more difficult for everyone when the Covid Pandemic hit in early 2020. Ruth and her cohabitants were quarantined for their own safety.

Figure 18-1. Dan and Betsy at their wedding with Grandma Ruth.

Figure 18-2. Hiddy and Ruth attending the wedding celebration.

In 2021 Dan and Betsy came to Georgia for the first time since their son had been born in May, 2020. They came to introduce Grandma Ruth to her first great grandchild which she finally met in person at a park in East Cobb on a wintry, February day. It was love at first sight; Ruth was smitten (Figure 18-4).

Unfortunately, the next day Ruth fell in her apartment and broke her nose and neck in two places (the day before her 96th birthday). She was transported to the hospital and, following her release, re-habbed in another facility for several weeks of physical therapy.

The kids had come from New York to celebrate Grandma's birthday with her, but she was now confined and quarantined in a nursing facility that prevented the family from seeing her for an extended period of time.

Ruth did make a remarkable recovery and when she moved back to her former residence, she moved into their Assisted Living unit. She

Figure 18-3. Entire family at Dan and Betsy's wedding (save a few).

Figure 18-4. Ruth, now a great grandmother, Finn, and his proud father, Dan.

continued to improve and regained most of her strength and mobility. The only difference was she now required a walker to get around.

The last few months of 2021, two significant family members passed away. Rube Babich, Edie's dear husband, died at 98, in late September. Now, Edie and Rube, the two star-struck lovers, are finally together again—for eternity.

In November, Ruth's close family experienced yet another loss. One of Hiddy's sons, Jack Gernsheimer (Jeff's identical twin brother,

Sharon's older brother, Nancy's Wolff's beloved husband), died from complications exacerbated by his Parkinson's Disease. He had fought bravely from this debilitating illness for 15 years. Jack will always be remembered for his kindness, generosity and his loving, gentle manner. He was a genuine mensch (Yiddish for a genuinely wonderful person).

The loss of a loved one's life is a forever ache in many ways. Ruth is the last one standing in her immediate family. Though it is a challenge to go on sometimes without those that she loved and grew up with, she has learned to persevere. Ruth still feels the presence of those she has lost and the love that she shared with each one of them.

Ruth is here to say that she is still vibrant and kicking. Despite the pandemic, which has changed life for everyone in many ways, she still prays (but not at the synagogue right now) for a better, kinder world. She still finds solace in prayer and in her faith.

She continues to strive to be the kind of person that inspires her family and friends as well. She says she has to work at it—at her age it doesn't come easily—but she is still committed to doing her part.

Hiddy used to say, "It's a great life, if you don't weaken." Ruth has no deliberate intention of weakening!

There's no doubt that she has been challenged from time to time throughout her long life; however, she still participates in exercise each day; plays Scrabble, bridge, and Rummy-Q; and keeps on going. Before she broke her neck, she was even crocheting waterproof mats for the homeless from plastic grocery bags that measured some 7 feet long!

She confines herself to soft acrylic yarn now, but still crochets. As a matter fact, one of Edie and Rube's grandchildren had a baby girl last year and named her Ilse (after Ruth's, Edith's, and Hilde's late little sister). Ruth was so absolutely touched by the honor and pride she felt for "little Ilse" and her parents that she crocheted an extra special baby blanket and matching bonnet for her.

Ruth celebrated her 97th birthday with her entire family on February 25, 2022!

On April 20, 2022 her dear brother-in-law, Harry Heinemann, passed away from his serious heart condition. Ruth wanted so badly to attend his grandson's wedding in late June in Madison, WI. She wanted to be there to lend her support and visit with the family after their significant loss and to enjoy the festivities that were planned for her great nephew and his beautiful bride.

Figure 18-5. Ruth with Hannah and Jakob Heinemann at their wedding in June of 2022 in Madison, WI.

Susan and Julie planned to fly to the celebration and, once Ruth decided to attend, arrangements were made for her to accompany them! She was by far the "guest of honor" along with the couple's grandparents. Everyone was so thrilled and delighted that Ruth felt well enough to make the trip at 97! The family truly enjoyed the wonderful "mitzvah" (great occasion) together (Figure 18-5).

Finally, it is with a deep sense of satisfaction that Ruth has come to appreciate the impact she still has on her family. She remains an important part of each one of her family members' lives (young and old). She keeps up with their progress and encourages them to reach for greater heights. She is an inspiration to all.

Now that David, her eldest grandson, has moved back to Georgia permanently, Ruth gets to see him regularly. After Ruth was forced to quarantine at her living facility due to the Covid pandemic in early 2020, Susan and Steve suggested she move into their home for a while. David, who was living in New York City at the time, joined them with his cat, and they all lived together for about 4 months. David and Ruth had always had a wonderful relationship, but it became even more special after they all lived under one roof for four months. They formed their own mutual admiration society.

Ruth also has so much love and affection for Dan, Betsy and Finn. She is in touch with them by phone weekly and they send her digital pictures on her "ever-changing" digital picture frame. That way, she can keep up with the little fella's adventures.

Figure 18-6. Susan Berman, Ruth Heinemann, and Adina Langer at the Tragedy of the St. Louis Exhibit. (Courtesy of Adina Langer, Curator, Kennesaw State University Museum of History and Holocaust Education.)

Figure 18-7. Ruth's great grandson with his grandfather, Steve Berman, pointing to the Simon family picture in front of which he is standing.

In early 2022, the Kennesaw State Museum of History and Holocaust Education mounted an exhibit on the "Tragedy of the St. Louis". This exhibit depicts the story of the Holocaust, the St. Louis, and the Simon family's experience (Figure 18-6). Figure 18-7 shows little Finn, Ruth's great grandson, visiting the display with his Grandpa

Figure 18-8. Ruth shares the glory of bubbles with the little guy on her 97th birthday.

Steve at age 1 1/2. It's never too early to begin to share the story, even in an elementary way.

Needless to say, Ruth loves spending time with her great grandson, Finn. Ruth is enjoying recapturing her youth through the eyes of her great grandson. She joins him on her 97th birthday as they go bubble popping (Figure 18-8). She now takes one day at a time and relishes each and every one.

Epilogue

There are some things that I would like to further clarify from the context of the previous pages.

One of those clarifications is just how we obtained the precious letters that my mother, Ruth, wrote to the Mizrahis (you'll notice a different spelling from the original letters). My mother was not aware at the time just how to spell their name and inserted a "c" into their last name. She was just learning English back in 1939.

Salim and Estrea Mizrahi had moved to Jacksonville, FL from Atlantic City, NJ sometime in the 1910's. Salim was a tailor and also sold fine linens. He and Estrea had six children. They joined a Conservative synagogue and opened a dry goods store that sold women's and children's clothing.

They were members of the same synagogue as my Great Tante Else (Meyerhoff) and were present when she made her impassioned appeal to the congregation for sponsors for her nieces and nephew in Europe. The Mizrahi's, being devoted to Judaism and wanting to help save Jews from the Nazi Regime and the Holocaust, graciously agreed to provide affidavits for Else's relatives.

Julie was one of the Mizrahi daughters and married Henry Halpern and lived in Jacksonville as well. They had three children. One of their daughters, Linda Halpern, married Michael Weinroth.

The Weinroths were married in the same synagogue as their family had always belonged to in Jacksonville and not only knew Else Meyerhoff as a friend, but had engaged her to cater their wedding.

My husband Steve and I met the Weinroths shortly after we moved to Marietta, GA in 1979—they had moved to Atlanta in the early 1970s and helped start a Conservative synagogue called Congregation Etz Chaim. Linda became the Education Director of the synagogue's Hebrew school, which my sons and her children, Adam and Traci, attended for their Jewish education.

When Linda had completed her 12th year as the Education Director, the congregation wanted to honor her in a befitting manner, so one Shabbat morning in the summer of 1988 a special Saturday morning service was held.

At the Oneg (Kiddish luncheon) that followed, I proceeded to introduce myself to Linda's parents and her Aunt Molly Mizrahi who had accompanied them from Jacksonville for the occasion. That is when Linda's Aunt said to me, "I believe I have some letters from some of your relatives from England that were sent to my parents before those girls came to America."

That's when I realized that Linda's grandparents had been the benevolent individuals who had sponsored my mother and aunt by providing them with the necessary affidavits to emigrate to America.

Not only, it appears, are we indebted to the Mizrahi family for their sponsorship of my mother and Aunt Hiddy, but we believe my late Aunt Edie; my mother's cousin, Ernest Ries; and my Great Uncle Meinhard's lives were also spared because of their generosity of spirit and compassion. They took a leap of faith because they believed in Tante Else and Uncle Albert's dedication to their Jewish faith and their love for their imperiled family in Europe.

My mouth flew open as Molly explained that she still had those letters back at home in Jacksonville and would send them to Linda when she returned to Florida. Those letters, as seen in Chapter 10 of this book, were written back in 1939 and 1943 and were given back to our family in Congregation Etz Chaim (which incidentally translates to Tree of Life) in the Rabbi's office a few days later!

I was delighted to receive them and made copies for our family and sent the originals to the US Holocaust Museum in Washington, DC. They are available online now for everyone to enjoy in my mother's own youthful handwriting.

I also want to include a subsequent occasion when Linda and I participated in a ceremony where together we laid a cobblestone in Etz Chaim's Holocaust Memorial Garden that was under construction at the time. A family in the Congregation, who had relatives that had perished in the war, was able to arrange for the synagogue to obtain railroad ties removed from railways that had led to the notorious Concentration Camp Treblinka, as well as several dozen cobblestones from the streets of the infamous Warsaw Ghetto, through the generosity of the US Holocaust Memorial Museum in Washington, D.C.

Linda and I were preparing to lift one of the cobblestones together to place in the cement walkway surrounding the Holocaust Memorial. Only, neither of us had any idea how heavy the stone was--its must have weighed in excess of 40 lbs. It took all our strength to lay it in front of the fountain in the beautiful garden that was designed to honor victims of the Shoah.

The irony was not lost on Linda or me that we were privileged to participate in the establishment of this significant Holocaust memorial. Linda represented her family who helped liberate and save many Holocaust victims, and I represented my family that had been the recipient of those individuals that they had saved—and we were both on American soil, thank G'd. We were both descendants of Abraham and our Jewish faith had brought us together.

Another story I wanted to share with my readers was the sheer coincidence that occurred in a grocery parking lot near my home. One day I happened to go to the local supermarket and, as I was locking my car, I heard a voice from the woman in the next parking space. She said something like, "This parking lot is surely a mess—and considering it is a grocery store, they ought to be ashamed of its condition."

I had never seen the woman before, but she had an accent. She sounded French and I asked her if she was from France? She said she was and I told her that currently we were living next door to a couple that was also from France.

We started to chat and I told her that I was a people collector. She inquired what that was and I told her it was my own way of getting to know people that I was fond of and keeping them in my heart. I asked her if she knew many people from France in the area and she said, "No." So, I suggested she might want to meet my neighbors. I guess she thought that that was a bit odd, but I explained that I was the daughter of immigrants and I had an affinity towards people from foreign countries.

We talked a little more and I began to tell her a little of my mother's story and when I got to the part about the voyage on the St. Louis, she stopped me. She said, "I don't believe it." I said, "What don't you believe—that it ever happened?"

"No," she said. She told me that she was currently reading a book about the St. Louis and was almost done. "Your story sounds a lot like the book I have been reading called, *The German Girl*." I told her that I had never heard of the book, but she insisted that I had to read it when she was done.

We exchanged phone numbers and subsequently got together. We met at a local restaurant and had lunch and she brought the book with her and handed it to me. Here we were, two nearly total strangers: She was French, I was American, meeting in a Mexican restaurant while she handed me *The German Girl* written by a Spanish author! Only in America!

While I was reading the book, about a week later, I happened to notice some pictures in the back. I thought it was probably ludicrous of me to look to see if I recognized any of our family, but I looked anyway. Incredibly, there was a picture of a group of young children about the ages of 9 to 11 or 12, and my Aunt Ilse was in the picture. I looked to see if she had been identified, but there were only a few children that were named under the picture. I was stunned to say the least and called my new-found friend up right away. Then I called Mom to tell her I had something incredible to show her.

The next day I took the book with me to see Mom and she confirmed that it was Ilse in the picture. She had never seen that picture before. How is that for a chance encounter!

It reminded me of when we had met Gottfried Bohmann on the street the day we went to Cloppenburg back in 2007, and he knew who we were from our last name!

I hope this story has enlightened you more about the Holocaust and how our family has been affected by it for generations. It is a tale of tragedy, loss and triumph at the same time.

There is one observation that occurs to me as I conclude this epic story of my mother's life and family. Isn't it both interesting and ironic that the word Kinder (German for children pronounced with a short "i"—rhyming with the word tinder) is spelled the same way as the word kinder (meaning gentle and full of goodness in English).

I believe it is not so much of a coincidence as it is thought provoking: If only the world had been kinder—*and evil had not prevailed*—there would not have ever been a need for a Kindertransport.

In Edie's Own Words

In March of 2022 while going through some papers of my Uncle Rube's, my cousin Sandy discovered a letter that my Aunt Edie had written back in April of 1977. Edie was describing the ordeal she and her family had been through to that point. Please note that this book was based on Ruth's memories of events, so you will see some small discrepancies in Edie's recollections. This letter was addressed to a friend of Edie's and is included here, in a somewhat abbreviated form.

My parents, my three sisters, and I lived in a small town of about 15,000 people with the name of Cloppenburg (near Oldenburg) in northwest Germany. My father was a horse dealer and I was the oldest of four girls.

We all went to Hoerere Maedchenschule in Cloppenburg, which was run by nuns. Being that I was the oldest, I was able to finish school. My sisters, however, weren't allowed to finish and went the last few years to the Jewish school in Oldenburg. It was an hour away by train.

The year of 1937 to 1938 from June to June I went to a finishing school called "das Paulinenstift" in Hamburg.

On November 10, 1938, the "Kristal Night", my father was arrested like all the other Jewish men in town. We had a small Jewish community in Cloppenburg with our own synagogue which was burned down by the Nazis that night.

My sister, Ruth, had already left by train for school but when she got there, the school was already in flames, etc.

My father was sent to a concentration camp near Berlin, Oranienburg where he was a prisoner for four weeks. In the meantime, my sisters, Ruth and Hilde (who were 13 and 12) were sent to England on the Kindertransport. They were very lucky. Ruth and Hilde were put in a home in Harrogate, England where they attended school and later learned their trades.

When my father was released from the camp, my parents started making arrangements to leave Germany for Cuba. We all had affidavits for America. My aunt and uncle from my hometown had made it and left Germany for Cuba and consequently told us to come there, too.

My parents booked passage for themselves and my youngest sister, Ilse, on a freighter called the Iller for Cuba. My papers hadn't come through when my parents wanted to leave. I was supposed to go with a family to England and be their house daughter, but my parents cancelled their plans and booked passage on the MS St. Louis instead so I could go with them.

We put some of our things on the Iller, the freighter, before it left so we could retrieve them when we landed in Cuba. We sailed on the St. Louis on May 13,1939. My parents had a cabin and I shared a cabin with my sister, Ilse. My two sisters stayed in England and were going to join us in America later.

Ilse was 11 and I was almost 17 then. Going to Cuba we were all happy and relieved to finally leave Germany. We had parties on board the ship every night.

However, when we came to Cuba, we couldn't land there. Instead, we had police guarding us on the ship and no one could get off. Everyone was terribly upset, putting it mildly.

My uncle, who was already in Cuba, came with his small boat, to shout to us, mañana (tomorrow) you'll come off, but mañana never came. My little sister would run all around shouting to my uncle "get us off," but no such luck. I remember the incident when a man cut his wrist and jumped overboard.

Finally we were told to go into a neutral zone near Miami and wait and see what could be done. A few passengers formed a committee to negotiate with the Captain to get us off the ship so we wouldn't have to return to Germany.

My parents sent wires daily to my sisters in England telling them what was happening. Finally, we were told we were returning to Europe. The captain was very nice to the passengers. He assured us he'd try everything not to send us back to Germany, and he kept his promise.

England, Holland, France, and Belgium promised to take in the passengers of the St. Louis, thank G'd. Being my sisters were already in England, we requested to go there too, but it was booked at once. So, our second choice was Holland because we had relatives there, too.

We were transferred into a small boat at Antwerp, Belgium and went to Holland. There we were put into a quarantine camp in Rotterdam. I remember sharing a barrack with other young girls. My parents were in a different barrack. On July 1st, that summer, I celebrated my 17th birthday in the camp.

In the meantime, I wrote to the people in Coventry, England and explained my story. I asked if I could still come to them. Luckily, the answer was, "yes." My parents got a pass and took me to the depot and put me on a train in Amsterdam with some other children, which came through Holland, heading for England.

That was the last time I ever saw my dear parents and sister, Ilse. Ilse was the only one they had left from us four girls, and so they didn't want to send her away, too. After a while, my parents and sister lived free with my aunt and cousin, but when Holland was overrun by Hitler, they were sent to Westerbork and later shipped from there with my sister to the gas chambers in Sobibor Concentration Camp in Poland.

In England, I stayed with my sponsors for about 1 1/2 years. I arrived there at the end of August just before the war broke out. I had it very good in Coventry. I shared a room with the daughter of the house and worked with her in their store and booths at the marketplace. I was also able to visit my two sisters in Harrogate and was happy to see them again.

In 1940 I got my visa to immigrate to the United States. My sisters had a high waiting number and couldn't go with me yet. But, four weeks before I sailed, I visited with them and stayed at the place where they lived. While I was there, Coventry was bombed and I never heard from my sponsors again.

I sailed for America and arrived here in November of 1940. My mother had a sister and family in Jacksonville, FL where I went to live.

My Uncle (Julius) got some of our things off the lift (storage) in Cuba and was able to save a few documents, pictures, and such. Uncle Julius, Tante (aunt) Selma and their son, Gunther, had papers come through for the United States. They moved to America to a small town in Illinois, only 13 miles from where I live now.

After living and working in Jacksonville for one year, I learned about my aunt and uncle from Cuba living in IL. They offered to send me to beauty school and pay for my training. I jumped at the opportunity. This would give me a chance to save money and bring my two sisters from England to the U.S.

After I received my license, I got a job in a local beauty parlor. I tried to save money to bring my two remaining sisters here. My aunt and I had to go to Washington, D.C. to a hearing at the State Department because my sisters were originally from Germany. Being it was April, 1944 and America was at war, the government took no chances. But they were cleared without any problem.

The weekend after we returned from Washington, D.C. a wonderful thing happened to me. A friend of mine and I went to Rockford to a U.S.O. dance. Camp Grant was located in Rockford and we attended the U.S.O. functions often. It was a formal dance no less and I looked like "Alice Blue Gown". (That refers to a song that was popular around that time.)

A soldier asked me to dance and saw my name, Edith Simon, so he said "a Yiddishe maidele" (a Jewish young woman)? I said, "yes," and asked him, "are you a Jewish boy?" He replied, "yes" and that's how I met my husband.

Rube was supposed to play (he was a musician) at the dance that night; he played the saxophone and the clarinet. The next day he pulled guard duty, but somehow got off and met me instead. Our courtship was a hectic one.

I took Rube home to meet my uncle and aunt who liked him a lot. In turn, he took me to his home in Brooklyn, NY to meet his folks on his last furlough at the end of May. When we came to Brooklyn, his sister and family were home, but Rube's parents had gone to the Catskill Mountains for a vacation over Memorial Day weekend.

We called his mother (I call her Mom) and she told us to come by bus to the country, which we did. Mom met us at the bus depot. When she saw me, I am blonde with blue eyes, she asked me "Are you a Nazi?" Then when I told her of course not and told my story, she was convinced her son was safe. Mom and Pop were the dearest people you can imagine, good and warmhearted, and we hit it off well at once. Mom, G'd bless her, who is 85 (as I write) is very smart and alert and could be a lawyer to this day. Pop, at that time, had a suit and coat factory, he was a contractor. I am sorry to say he died about 10 years ago.

Anyhow, Rube had his last furlough then and we went back to IL together and June 6 he sailed overseas. As luck had it, he was sent to England where he had a chance to visit my sisters for the High Holidays. He also looked up another three to four cousins of mine.

We corresponded (Rube and me) daily and made tentative wedding plans for his return. In the meantime, my two sisters finally got their visa to come here in January, 1945. I went to New York to meet them and stayed at Rube's parents house, who were just great.

I brought my sisters to IL then and both Ruth and Hilde got jobs here in Freeport. Hilde and I were both beauticians and shared an apartment. Ruth was a saleslady and stayed at my aunt and uncle's home.

The letters were flying across the ocean to Rube and vice versa. In the Spring of 1945, he said he'd be coming home soon for a furlough but would have to go on to the Pacific then. He had asked me to come to NY and we would get married. So, again, my sisters and I packed up and left for NY. It was July by then.

Both my sisters got good jobs and an apartment in Brooklyn. Rube finally arrived home on Saturday, July 21st, and believe it or not, on July 24th, Tuesday evening, we were married. It was a small wedding across the street from Rube's house in a little shul (synagogue).

We had a nice honeymoon, but the best thing that happened was V-J Day, the war ended. We had block parties every night and the mood was exuberant. As luck would have it, Rube didn't have to go on to the Pacific and instead was stationed at a camp in Alabama. I followed him. We had a room in a boarding house and the honeymoon continued.

In January 1946 we went back to NY and I became a United States citizen, which was another highlight of my life. I was already expecting our first baby by then.

After that, Rube was stationed near NY for a while and also got his discharge from the Army that winter. Our oldest daughter, Sandy, was born in 1946. Later, we had two more daughters: Karen in 1949 and Janice in 1951.

Rube meanwhile worked very hard to make a living for his "four girls". He worked two jobs and went to school, New York University, at night. He finally got his diploma as an accountant in 1952. He got a nice job as an office manager in the garment district in Manhattan.

We had a nice apartment in Mom and Pop's two-family house. We lived there for 15 years. In 1960, however, we bought a split level house out on Long Island.

Our girls grew up and started college. Meanwhile, Rube became a stamp dealer, which was his hobby. He turned it into his business. This was a lucky break, things started looking rosier.

Our oldest daughter, Sandy, got married in 1967 and moved out here to Freeport, IL, where my story practically began. We started visiting her and her husband at least one or two times a year, especially when they started to have children.

In 1973 we decided to move out to Freeport, too. By then, our second daughter, Karen, was married and raising her child. Janice, the youngest, was also away from home.

We got a lovely house around the corner from our children and we like it very much here.

Rube and I do a lot of traveling still, by car. He mostly buys stamps at auctions in the East and we attend a lot of shows and exhibits. This brings you up to date.

Sincerely,
Edie

Acknowledgments

It's hard to remember how many countless people I have told my mother's family history to who have said, "This should be written down somewhere". It began to occur to me that they were right; I ought to write it down. The more I told the story, the more I began to envision the way I would shape it on paper.

I also began to appreciate how very fortunate we were to have my mother and her sisters in our lives, considering the circumstances through which they had lived. They deserved to have their history recorded for their children, grandchildren, great-grandchildren, and posterity because they had sacrificed so much to rebuild their lives out of so much tragedy and loss.

The former Simon sisters (my mother Ruth and late Aunts Edie and Hiddy) are the heroines of this story along with their parents; our beloved late grandparents, Karl and Selma Simon; and their youngest sister, our dear, late Aunt Ilse. My beloved grandparents and Ilse were murdered by a heinous, barbaric maniac and his followers for what reason … because society turned a blind eye to justice and human decency and because they were Jewish!

Without question I want to thank my mother for bestowing in me the courage to take this project on. Your inspiration means so much to me and I thank you from the bottom of my heart for sharing your history, your courage, and your faith with me. I am also indebted to my wonderful late father, Fred, who taught me so much about life, love, and perseverance.

My beloved late aunts, Edie and Hiddy, deserve significant recognition for their warm affection and the examples they set for me growing up. They were each beautiful, accomplished women with exceptionally generous spirits that helped raise me, my sister, and my cousins with hearts full of love. All three sisters taught me what it means to be a good sister.

My staunchest supporter and love of my life, my wonderful husband, Steve Berman, deserves a lot of credit for all the weeks, months, and years he has had to tolerate my weariness and fatigue that working on this manuscript frequently manifested. He knew how much this story meant to me and the family, so he kept encouraging me and reading and rereading my revisions countless times.

My terrific sons David and Daniel Berman, and my talented, wonderful daughter-in-law, Betsy Steed, fill my heart with love and joy. My heart sings when I am with my little Finn; thank you for him. May he know only kindness and acceptance throughout his blessed long lifetime.

My dear sister, Julie, and her amazing husband, Rich, have walked with me on this journey, too. Their love and affection for our family is clearly evident in everything they do, and can always be counted on no matter the circumstances. Thank you for being the remarkable people you are.

Thank you to the most compassionate individuals that took care of my late brother, Gary, after he was relocated from Willowbrook. He had a gentle soul and your words of beauty describing his courage, patience, and acceptance brought our family a deeper understanding of how much he gave to others. Linda Klingbeil, we are so grateful to you for your devotion to Gary and our entire family. In addition, I like to reiterate our thanks to Uncle Harry and Aunt Susan Heinemann for the many ways they looked after my blessed brother when he was alive.

To my first cousins—the late, adored Jack Gernsheimer and his brother and sister, Jeff and Sharon; Sandy, Karen, and Janice; and

Richard Heinemann and their spouses, thank you for sharing our rich family history. You each have encouraged me and helped me piece this puzzle of our past generations with letters, pictures, and recollections of your own.

Jeff is responsible, by the way, for the beautifully designed front and back covers of this book. I know that you are proud, Jeff, to carry the torch that your late mother, Hiddy, lit when she started speaking to children and adults about our family's history many years ago.

My maternal second cousins also have been extremely supportive and shared information they supplied me. They would be Ellen, Vera, Mark, Diana, David, Patty, Steve, Jeannie, and Martha, along with Harriet and her beloved late husband, my mother's first cousin, Eric Meyerhoff, in Savannah, Georgia. Eric was Tante Else and Uncle Albert's son.

My earliest volunteer editors were Marc and Suzy Zemel and Linda Weinroth. Countless hours went into reading, rewriting, and gently correcting my "errors in eras." Thank you for all your hard work, patience, and questions to improve my grammar, spelling, and punctuation.

Once again thank you from the bottom of all our hearts to Linda Weinroth and her loving grandparents, the Mizrahi family, who without their involvement in our family's lives, none of this would have been possible.

I want to show my family's gratitude to Rabbi C. Simon, my mother's former Boynton Beach, Florida Rabbi, who so kindly wrote the Foreword for this book. His well-crafted words set the tone for the rest of the manuscript.

Thank you to Laurette Rondenet and Gail Scott for allowing me to share the history of my father's career with your company, Edlong Corporation. Laurette, your father, Gene Rondenet, and Jack Bremner, the founders of the company, were so very generous to our family during my father's employment and after he retired. We will always be grateful to you.

To Lauren Biddle Plummer, my "professional" editor, who has been enlightening in her editing of this manuscript and supportive from the start. She will continue to provide me with guidance as we wish to do an e-version of this publication as well. Thank you for being patient with me and my "technological challenges." You've taught me so much.

I'd like to acknowledge the wonderful staff at the Kennesaw State University's Museum of History and Holocaust Education in Kennesaw, Georgia. Adina Jocelyn Langer, Curator of the Museum, in particular, has done exemplary work in promoting Holocaust education and developing Holocaust curriculum, programs, and exhibits for years. Dr. Catherine M. Lewis, Assistant Vice President and Director of the Museum has been very generous to our family in presenting our story to the public through "The Tragedy of the St. Louis" exhibit.

Also many thanks to James Newberry, Special Projects Curator, and Tyler Crafton-Karnes, Adult Program Coordinator and Accessibility Specialist, who were significantly involved in the taping of the testimonial I gave initially to the Museum a few years ago as well as the coordination and promotion of the St. Louis traveling exhibit. More information can be found at Georgia Journeys exhibit: https://georgiajourneys.kennesaw.edu/tours/show/33.

Institutions and museums like KSU's Museum of History and Holocaust Education, the United States Holocaust Memorial Museum in Washington, DC, The William Bremen Heritage Museum in Atlanta and, the-soon-to-be renovated Anne Frank Museum in Sandy Springs, Georgia inspire me. It is comforting to know that stories of the Holocaust will prevail to teach us all invaluable lessons of the dangers of intolerance, prejudice, anti-Semitism, racism, homophobia, xenophobia, and bigotry in society.

Right now there is a war going on in Ukraine. Thank goodness that most countries (including our own, the United States) are beginning to take the poor Ukrainians that had to flee because of Russia's despot Putin and his aggressive Russian Army. Will the need for more power and greed never stop?

Granted, the Ukrainian people in general were not very kind to the Jews that left Germany and other countries during WWII. But surprisingly, there is a large population of Jewish people in Ukraine today. Apparently, the country has been more accepting of them and even their new President is Jewish—Volodymyr Zelenskyy. May peace come to the region soon.

When I started writing this book in 2018 it was before the Covid Pandemic, the 2020 election, the insurrection at the US Capitol, and the invasion of Ukraine. As I compose my thoughts today, in 2022, these serious issues are playing in the back of my mind along with climate change, poverty, immigration, inflation, and the thought of world dominance by tyrants in our midst. May men and women from every part of the planet come together to help solve these complex problems. *Together* we will be strong—*together* we will find solutions and learn to live in harmony with one another.

I apologize for digressing, but I felt the need to express my thoughts on the subject of intolerance. Which leads me to my next question…

What would the world be like if we didn't have friends? My friends, too numerous to mention because I am a "people collector," shall go unnamed … but you know who you are and I love each of you. They have shown interest in my project, encouraged me and spurred me on to greater heights. Your love and affection for me and my family, particularly my mother, have humbled and touched me deeply.

Thank you also to the Atlanta Jewish Family and Career Services for the hard work and devotion the organization shows our community in general, and especially the Holocaust survivors in their midst. They have wonderful programs for these seniors and provide counseling and designated funds for those who qualify to help defray their medical services and medication. They are all caring individuals and I would especially like to acknowledge the hard work of Amy Neumann, Anat Granath, Keryn Benasuly, and Cherie Aviv.

One more thank you goes to Dana Wachsmann. She is a good friend of the family and is a volunteer in the One Deed program, also affiliated with the Atlanta Jewish Family and Career Services. She has been and is a delightful companion, confidant, and a great help to me and my mother. Thank you, Dana, you have made such a difference in our lives and are part of our family now.

I'd like to personally thank the citizenry of Cloppenburg, Germany for generously inviting our family back to Germany to honor our relatives lost in the War. Thank you for engaging the artisan that installed the Stolpersteine in your community memorializing our family and your other former Jewish residents. Also, to those individuals who went out of their way to show compassion and generosity like Anja Wienken and her family and Gottfried and Christa Bohmann, you have touched our lives forever.

When our family went back to Cloppenburg in 2010 for the dedication ceremony for the Stolpersteine, we met a young teacher by the name of Anja Westerhoff. Subsequently, she reached out to my cousins and me for information about our family. She wanted to work with her students to put a project together regarding the Simon family story. The name of the technical school in Cloppenburg that is responsible for this project is BBS Technik.

We are most appreciative of their sharing our family history with their students and the community at large. Thank you Anja, to your classes, and to your institution for discussing and presenting such a wonderful display. It is so important that the message continues to be delivered. There are new generations, and old ones, too, that must never deny what took place. There is a lovely message and tribute to my late Aunt Ilse that, I hope, is still available to be viewed on youtube. Here is the link: https://www.youtube.com/watch?v=ywnmDsP0dJg

I wish to thank the United States Holocaust Memorial Museum in Washington, DC for its continued devotion and contribution to the dissemination of material and programs promoting the truth about the Holocaust. Thank you for all the help you provided me in researching and incorporating the many pictures in my book.

I also want to acknowledge a wonderful woman named Pamela Sampson who was kind enough to reach out to me some time ago to give me permission to use quotations from the book she authored called, *No Reply: A Jewish Child Aboard the MS St. Louis and the Ordeal That Followed.* Henry Gallant was the gentleman that dictated the story of his life to Pamela and shared his experiences on the St. Louis as a ten-year-old boy.

Also, I want to acknowledge Martin Goldsmith and his novel, *The Inextinguishable Symphony,* that gave me insight into the city of Oldenburg and what occurred during the Kristallnacht roundup of my grandfather and thousands of other Jewish men like him.

Thank you, too, to Bea Green for your generosity for sharing how the Kindertransport program started in England. The ongoing organizations of the KTA, The Kindertransport Association, here in America, and the AJR, The Association of Jewish Refugees, in England, connects Kinder and their families with one another. They reach around the world to support and highlight the good work that is associated with many refugee organizations helping displaced people today.

One other individual that has been in touch with us the last couple of years is a gentleman and teacher named Klaus Erdmann. He was instrumental (pardon the pun) in presenting a memorial concert and presentation in conjunction with a memorial march that took place in Oldenburg, Germany on Kristallnacht back in 2019. The town conducts the march each year on November 10th, but that year there was a musical accompaniment. The English translation of the German piece performed that year is "Nobody is Forgotten; Nothing Has Been Forgotten." Klaus commented when he sent us documentation of the event that as the music was performed "the Simon family story has been told and will be remembered by many." We thank you and your colleagues for this honor and for remembering to continue to tell the story of the Holocaust across the country and around the world in the hopes of reminding us all that we must *Never Forget*.

Thank you to you, the reader, of *Challenging Faith* that have purchased this book and continue to share our family's story. We are counting on all of you to spread the word that ***None of Us Must Ever Forget***.